MY BIBLE 101

A Condensed Bible Reference for New Christians

Sandy Butcher

My Bible 101: A Condensed Bible Reference for New Christians

Trilogy Christian Publishers A Wholly Owned Subsidary of Trinity Broadcasting Network

2442 Michelle Drive Tustin, CA 92780

Cover design by: Grant Swank

For information about special discounts for bulk purchases, please contact Trilogy Christian Publishing.

Trilogy Disclaimer: The views and content expressed in this book are those of the author and may not necessarily reflect the views and doctrine of Trilogy Christian Publishing or the Trinity Broadcasting Network.

Manufactured in the United States of America

10 9 8 7 6 5 4 3 2 1

Library of Congress Cataloging-in-Publication Data is available.

ISBN: 978-1-68556-653-1

E-ISBN: 978-1-68556-654-8

DEDICATED TO

Every new Christian who is inspired to want to know quickly about the history of the Bible, God, Jesus, and the Holy Spirit, to make it easier in church, Bible studies, serving, and just how to act in life as a new Christian.

ACKNOWLEDGMENTS

Thank you, Loreen Blume Edwards, for having the patience to edit the first draft of my manuscript.

Thank you, Creflo Dollar, for all the Bible teachings you taught me and for my ability to be able to write this condensed Bible book for new Christians.

Thank you, Joyce Meyer, for all the teachings on the Bible and how new Christians should present themselves after salvation.

Thank you, Journey Church Bible study group, for all your encouragement.

Thank you, Vic, my daughter, for your encouragement and for keeping me humble.

Thank You, Lord, for giving me the purpose to write this book at eighty years old.

Thank You, Holy Spirit, for Your guidance, giving knowledge and wisdom, and the strength to write this book, making it all possible.

TABLE OF CONTENTS

PREFACE

I am so excited I finished this book for you as a new Christian. This is a condensed source of the Bible to help you in your new journey with God, Jesus the Son of God, and the Holy Spirit. I was inspired by a physical therapist after my back surgery. She was a new Christian, and the Holy Spirit put it in my heart at eighty years old to write a book to help her. The book became my new purpose, and I loved writing about the Bible with the Holy Spirit's guidance. I have always been very compassionate about knowing everything all at once.

Please take my hand and enjoy the lives of the Bible: the obedience, love, and mercy of God; Jesus Christ, our Savior who died at the cross, shed His blood for our sins and gave us eternal life; and the Holy Spirit, who guides, comforts, strengthens, gives us power, knowledge, and wisdom to help us through our daily lives.

OLD TESTAMENT

Now, let us start from the beginning and explain that God created everything, including the man and the woman, in six days and rested on the seventh, known as the Sabbath. God, the Son of God, and the Holy Spirit are known as the Trinity. All have been there before time began. Jesus was sent by God the Father to become flesh and was conceived by the Spirit in Mary's womb. Even as Jesus became a man, He did not give up His divinity, so He remained fully, one hundred percent, God. The Holy Spirit is one with God the Father and God the Son. You do not see Him, but Jesus placed the Holy Spirit inside you on the day of your salvation, and it was also through His power that Jesus was raised from the dead. He is there as your Comforter to provide an irreversible affirmation that we are God's. He teaches and transforms our hearts so that our affections and responses become increasingly like Jesus'. He guides us with knowledge and wisdom to try to make the right decisions the first time. I have found that if I am patient and wait for an answer to my problem, the first thing that comes into my head is usually the right one. God never wants to be second to anything or anyone.

Beginning at Genesis 1, when God created the heavens and earth, He formed man from the dust of the ground, breathed into his nostrils the breath of life, and man became a living being. God, to this day, creates life in each of our mother's wombs to become an image of Him. That is why we are all different, and God loves each one of us as His children. He is also a jealous God and does not want to share you. He expects you to be obedient and righteous. He gave us free will to do good or evil with the hope that we would all pick good. Evil is Satan's and occupies our carnal body, but our spiritual body is God's. You will find that all bad is from Satan. The earth is his home, so we need to be careful that we do not follow him with bad instructions being put in our ears. The Holy Spirit is at the beginning with God, hovering over the face of the waters.

God created Adam and Eve and told them they could eat of every tree in the Garden except for the Tree of Good and Evil, which they should not eat. They were both naked and not ashamed. Then the serpent, Satan, was more cunning than any beast of the field that the Lord God created. He said to Eve, as she was eating fruit in the Garden, "You will not surely die. For God knows that in the day you eat of it, your eyes will be opened, you will be like God, knowing good and evil" (Genesis 3:4–5). Both Adam and Eve realized when they ate of the Tree of Good and Evil, both of their eyes opened, they saw they were naked, and with God's help, they sewed fig leaves together and made themselves coverings. God called to them, and they said they heard God's voice but were afraid because they were naked, so they hid. Adam blamed Eve for eating of the tree. God told Eve, "I will greatly multiply your sorrow and your conception; in pain, you shall bring forth children; your desire shall be for your husband, and he shall rule over you" (Genesis 3:16). To Adam, He said, "Cursed is the ground for your sake; In toil, you shall eat of it all the days of your life" (Genesis 3:17).

Adam and Eve created the first sin in the Garden. We are subjected to being sinners every day of our lives because we cannot be perfect like Jesus. Adam and Eve begot Cain and Abel. Cain killed his brother, Abel. There was so much sin in those times. God told Noah to build an ark; He was going to flood the world, cleanse it, and then start over. So, Noah did what God said because he was so righteous to God. Noah took his wife, their sons, and their sons' wives. And of every living thing, he brought two, a male and a female. He was also to take seven each of every clean animal, a male and a female; also, seven each of birds of the air, male and female, to keep the species alive in the face of all the earth. After seven days, God called it to rain on the earth for forty days and forty nights. During that time, God destroyed from the face of the earth all living things that He had made. After leaving the ark, Noah built an altar to the Lord, took every clean animal and every clean bird, and offered burnt offerings on the altar. And the Lord smelled a soothing aroma. Then the Lord said in His heart, "I will never again curse the ground for man's sake, although the imagination of man's heart is evil from his youth, nor will I again destroy every living thing as I have done" (Genesis 8:21). "God blessed Noah and his sons and said to them: 'Be fruitful and multiply, and fill the earth'" (Genesis 9:1). Multiply to God means anything over two.

> Then God spoke to Noah and to his sons with Him, saying, "And as for Me, behold, I establish My covenant with you and with your descendants after you, and with

every living creature that is with you: the birds, the cattle, and every beast of the earth with you, of all that go out of the ark, every beast of the earth. Thus, I establish My covenant with you: Never again shall all flesh be cut off by the waters of the flood; never again shall there be a flood to destroy the earth."

Genesis 9:8–11

"And God said: 'This is the sign of the covenant which I make between you and Me and every living creature that is with you, for perpetual generations'" (Genesis 9:12). God set His rainbow in the cloud, and it was a sign of the covenant between Him and the earth. The rainbow to God is to remember the everlasting covenant between Him and every living creature of all flesh that is on the earth.

In the second covenant God made with Abram, He said, "To your descendants I have given the land, from the river of Egypt to the great river, the River of Euphrates" (Genesis 15:18). God promised Abram, at ninety-nine years old, a covenant between Him and Abram that he would multiply exceedingly. His descendants would be as many as there were stars in the sky and would be His descendants. He said He would make nations for them, twelve to be exact. Every male child was to be circumcised at the age of eight days old. This was the sign of the covenant between God and His children, the Israelites. If they did not receive circumcision, that person would be cut off from His people; they had broken the covenant.

God, changing Abram's name to Abraham, told Abraham to take his son, his only son, whom he loved, and go to the land of Moriah, offer him as a burnt offering on one of the mountains, of which God would tell him. Isaac questioned Abraham about the fire and the wood but no lamb for a burnt offering. Abraham told his son God would provide the lamb. Then they went to the place of which God had told him. He bounded his son and laid him on the altar, upon the wood. And Abraham stretched out his hand and took the knife to slay his son. But an angel of the Lord called to him from heaven and said, "Abraham, Abraham. Do not lay your hand on the lad or do anything to him." For now, God knew Abraham feared God since he had not withheld his son, his only son, from God. Then the angel of the Lord called to Abraham a second time out of heaven. The angel of the Lord said,

> "By Myself, I have sworn, says the Lord, because you have done this thing and have not withheld your son, your only son, blessings I will bless you, and multiplying I will multiply your descendants as the stars of the heaven and as the sand which is on the seashore; and your descendants shall possess the gate of their enemies. In your seed all the nations of the earth shall be blessed, because you have obeyed My voice."

Genesis 22:16–18

Sarai was Abraham's wife, whom God blessed. He changed her name to Sarah and told her she would be a mother of nations, and the kings of peoples all would come from her. God's people were the nations of Israel. Abraham had one son, Isaac, with Sarah. Isaac had twin boys with Rebekah, his wife; their names were Esau and Jacob. Isaac loved Esau because he ate off the game, but Rebekah loved Jacob. Jacob said to Esau, "Sell me your birthright as of this day." Esau felt he was to die anyway, so he figured, "What is this birthright to me?" Esau, from then on, despised his birthright.

Jacob, who God renamed Israel because he yielded his life to God's purpose, had twelve sons among all his wives. God gave Jacob the land of his father, Isaac, and his grandfather, Abraham.

Jacob's twelve sons were literally the children of "Israel." The Israelites knew that God would build them into a larger tribe. The term "children of Israel" came to signify the whole body of God's chosen, and it saved their people. It included Israel's grandchildren and all other members of his household. From here, they went to Egypt for a stay of four hundred and thirty years. While in Egypt, they grew from a clan of several hundred to a nation of almost 3 million.

Joseph was one of Jacob's twelve sons. He was favored by his father, who had given him a long robe that is usually worn by royalty. His brothers did not like him because he told them about his dreams of the sun and moon and the eleven stars that made them obedient to him. Jacob sent Joseph to feed the sheep with his brothers, but the brothers went to Dothan, so Joseph followed them.

When they saw Joseph, they conspired to slay him and throw him in a pit, but his brother Reuben heard it and delivered him out of their hands. Reuben said not to shed blood, cast him into this pit in the wilderness, and lay no hand upon him. His brothers stripped Joseph out of his coat and cast him in the pit with no water. The brothers sat down to eat their bread, and when they looked up, they saw a company of Ishmaelites from Gilead with all their wares to carry down to Egypt. The brothers, instead of the pit, decided to sell him to the Ishmaelites, but then the Midianite merchantmen went and instead lifted Joseph out of the pit, and they sold Joseph to the Ishmaelites for twenty pieces of silver, and they took Joseph into Egypt. When Reuben returned, Joseph was not in the pit, and he took his clothes. The brothers dipped the coat into goat's blood and told their father that Joseph was probably devoured by an evil beast. Jacob mourned for many days.

The Midianites sold Joseph in Egypt to Potiphar, an officer of the pharaoh and captain of the guard. Joseph received favor from the pharaoh, and the pharaoh made him ruler over all the land of Egypt except for the pharaoh's land.

For seven years, Joseph knew a famine was coming, so he gathered up all the food that was in the land of Egypt and stored it in the cities. Now, all of Egypt was in a famine, so Joseph sold all the food in the storehouses. All the countries in Egypt went to buy corn. Even Jacob and his sons, who wanted Joseph dead, went to buy corn.

Then, the pharaoh told Joseph to bring their whole family out of Canaan to Egypt to live, and they all moved. Joseph made the best of his situation as a slave in Egypt, earning the trust of his master—until his master's wife accused him falsely of assaulting her, and Joseph was quickly thrown in prison for two years. Joseph continued to rely on God, and he succeeded in any situation he found himself in. Joseph died at one hundred ten. Israel was still a large extended family that was settled in Goshen near Egypt.

As time went by, a new pharaoh thought the Israelites were growing too fast, and he was jealous. They grew into a large nation, so the new pharaoh enslaved them for four hundred and thirty years to work for the Egyptians. These were the Hebrews waiting for God to make them into a nation He had promised to their ancestor Abraham.

The pharaoh was afraid his slave nation was becoming too populated and too powerful, so he issued the order that all their male babies be slaughtered at birth. This was a major factor in the Hebrews crying out to God for deliverance, and He heard their cries. The mother of Moses put him in a basket so he would not be killed by the pharaoh. He floated down the river, and the pharaoh's daughter saw him. Moses became the leader God chose to speak to the Hebrews and the pharaoh on His behalf, and through Moses, God saved His people from their bondage after performing ten plagues, which did not worry the pharaoh until the last one. At that time, God's wrath killed all the firstborn male people of Egypt. This included all beasts.

On the first month and the tenth day, the people, according to their number, were to bring an unblemished, yearling lamb or goat. They were to keep it up for fourteen days of the same month, and the killing would be in the evening. Afterward, they would take the blood and strike the lamb or goat on the two side posts and on the upper door post of the house where they ate. The meat, including the innards, was to be roasted and eaten with unleavened bread with bitter herbs. This meal is what kept the Israelites healthy, free from all illnesses while in the wilderness for forty years. This day was to be a memorial, and they would keep it as a feast to the Lord throughout their generations.

Egypt was not as powerful as God in fulfilling His covenant promise to Abraham and the Hebrew people. He broke the bonds of slavery in Egypt, and Moses led His people via the Red Sea, where it was parted by God so they could walk on dry land. Then God drowned all the Egyptians, chariots, and horses when He closed the Red Sea. The people went into the wilderness to meet Him in preparation for becoming a great nation to represent Him to the entire world. God is always faithful, loving, and merciful in His promises and people, no matter how difficult the situation might seem. All you need to do is cry out to Him. This is still true today.

After the death of the great pharaoh, God appeared to Moses in a burning bush at Mount Sinai and commissioned him to deliver the enslaved people out of the land of Egypt. Here, God extended His covenant with Abraham and Jacob to embrace the whole nation of the sons of Israel, promising, "Now if you obey Me fully and keep My covenant then out of all nations you will be My treasured possessions. Although the whole earth is mine, you will be for Me a kingdom of priests and a holy nation" (Exodus 19:5–6). God gave them salvation by officially adopting Israel as His own sons and daughters and on the atoning that Jesus Christ would someday suffer to redeem all of God's people.

Three days out of bondage and into the wilderness of Shur, they found only bitter water. The Lord showed them a tree to make the water sweet. Then they traveled to Elim, where there were twelve wells of water and many palm trees. When they left Elim, all the Israelites and their children went into the Wilderness of Sin. On the fifteenth day of the second month after departing Egypt, they began to murmur again against Moses and his older brother, Aaron. The people thought the Lord was killing them with hunger. The Lord told Moses He would rain manna (bread) from heaven and supply quail for them to eat for meat for their evening meal. Moses said unto them, "This is the bread which the Lord hath given you to eat" (Exodus 16:15). They ate the food the Lord provided for forty years in the wilderness. Always believe and trust that God will supply you with everything you need!

God revealed Himself to them through the Ten Commandments and the rest of the law at Mount Sinai. God wanted to set His people apart so that the entire world would recognize them as His people and would want to follow Him as well. But while Moses was meeting with God at Mount Sinai, the people began acting just like the nations by creating their own idols to worship!

While Moses was with God, God informed him to arise and get down from Mount Sinai and go to the people. They had corrupted themselves; they were quickly turning aside from God and the words

He had commanded them. This made God angry, and He called them stiff-necked. He wanted to destroy the Israelites. The Lord was very angry with Aaron for helping them. Moses took their sins, the bronze calf which they had made, burned it with fire, stamped it and grounded it as small as dust, and cast it all into the brook. Moses threw the tablets on the ground and broke them.

Moses stood at the entrance of the camp and said, "Whoever is on the Lord's side, come to me!" (Exodus 32:26). And all the sons of Levi gathered themselves together to him. And he said to them, "Let every man put his sword on his side, and go in and out the camp, and let every man kill his brother, every man his companion, and every man his neighbor" (Exodus 32:27). So the sons of Levi did as Moses said, and about three thousand men of the people fell that day. Then Moses said, "Consecrate yourselves today to the Lord, that He may bestow a blessing this day; for every man has opposed his son and his brother" (Exodus 32:29).

In the Old Testament, you can see God had to be a jealous God for such disobedience to Him. He does not want to be shared with anyone or anything. He also wants to be first in your family. He created you in your mother's womb, and He has numbered every hair on your head. He knows before you do anything what the results will be. Remember, He has given you free will to choose your own destiny, but He hopes you will listen to the Holy Spirit for the right directions. I have found that if I listen to the Holy Spirit, usually, the first nudge of my Spirit is what I should do. Doing the wrong things makes life much harder to endure, and many times, you are not successful.

You were put on this earth for a purpose. Every person has their own individual purpose, just as none of us look alike. We are all different. If you look at your life, you can possibly figure it out with help from Jesus and the Holy Spirit. Because you are a born-again Christian, Jesus gives you the Holy Spirit to help guide, comfort, and give you power and strength. I pray every day for the Holy Spirit to help me every minute.

We are never alone, and He will never leave us because He lives inside us. God is loving and merciful always, and Jesus died at the cross to take our sins and give us eternal life. God does not have to turn wrath on us for our sins. Jesus is our advocate to God because we could never be perfect like Jesus. If we cry out or ask anything, in Jesus' name, He will do it, but we must try to pray every day, thank Him for what He has done for us, read and study the Word so we will be informed, and want to serve in some manner. Jesus served through all His parables and ministry, so, us being servants, we need to do the same. "You shall love the Lord your God with all your heart, with all you soul, and with all your strength. This is the first commandment" (Mark 12:30).

Moses met God for forty days and forty nights, in the midst of a cloud, at the top of Mount Sinai, for God to give Moses two tablets to replace the original ones because they were destroyed by the disobedience of the Israelites while Moses was with God. God also gave them the tablets of the covenant.

God gave the Israelites His fundamental moral law, the Ten Commandments, together with other statutes, about 613.

He furnished them with His ceremonial law to depict Israel's reconciliation with their Heavenly Father and to provide a symbolic way of forgiveness.

Israel broke camp, they went to the southern border of the Promised Land, and God told them to go in and take possession. There were ten spies to make plans of how to take the nation, and out of all ten spies, eight decided not to go in because they thought they could not overthrow the giants who lived there. Only Joshua and Caleb were willing to go and overthrow the giants because they knew God had given them the Promised Land. After taking forty days in the desert spying, all the tribal representatives, except Joshua and Caleb, reported that it was unfavorable and decided to go against God's wishes. Moses' intercession did save them from God's wrath, but the Lord still condemned them for their disobedience. He condemned them to wander the forty years in the wilderness, one year for each day of spying until that entire generation died away.

After this, the advance of the Hebrews on Canaan resumed. Moses anointed Joshua as his successor, spoke two addresses, and then he ascended Mount Pisgah to view the Promised Land. There, Moses died. God buried him with His own hands. He had been the founder of the Hebrews, who were uncircumcised Jews, to be a nation.

As Joshua went forward to the land of Canaan, prepared for conquest by the Hebrews, they were crossing the Jordan River at flood stage, and Joshua knew God would open a gateway for them, which He did, so they would know He was God. They crossed the dry riverbed, led by the ark of God's testament. Joshua's wars of conquest included the central, southern, and northern Canaan. After seven years of battle, Israel gained control of the land, which was divided and allotted to the tribes. Each of the twelve tribes was given their own land, but they were to finish the job of driving out the Canaanites and take complete possession of the Promised Land on their own. Joshua continued to encourage the people to remain faithful to God so they could remain in the Promised Land, which was Israel's earthly inheritance. But Israel had a spiritual inheritance that we can share when we live a life of faithfulness to God.

The Levites were not given any land to possess since they were set apart to serve God and to be His own. Instead, they were given cities within the boundaries of the land given to other tribes. Some of these cities were designated as cities of refuge, where those accused of murder could flee and remain safe while awaiting trial.

There was still land that could be conquered, but Joshua was compelled by advancing age to divide the land they had among the twelve Hebrew tribes. Joshua led the Israelites to military victory. He then charged his people with faithfulness to the Lord and died. After his death, however, the tribes failed to clear the inhabitants from the land, so the Lord withdrew His promise to help drive the people out and bless the Israelites in battle. The new generation abandoned God and worshipped idols. This shows what can happen when we neglect to teach our children to follow the Lord.

The first generation failed to trust God to give them the Promised Land, and they died in the wilderness. The second one failed to complete the task of conquering the land, and they died defeated.

The third generation did not even remember the mighty things God had done for Israel.

They forsook the Lord and served Baal and Ashtaroth. And the anger of the Lord was so thoroughly against the Israelites that He delivered them into the hands of spoilers who spoiled them, and then He sold them into the hands of the enemies so that they could not stand positively before their enemies. The hand of the Lord was against them for evil, as the Lord had said, and as the Lord had sworn unto them, and they were greatly distressed.

Even the judges delivered them out of the hand of those who spoiled them, but they would not listen to their judges but continued to worship other gods and bowed themselves down to them. The Lord tried to keep them from corruptive lives, but they ceased not from their own doings nor from their stubborn ways.

The Lord was angered with the Israelites, and He said, "Because these people have transgressed My covenant which I commanded their fathers and have not listened to My voice, I also will not from this time forth drive out any from before them of the nations which Joshua left when he died" (Judges 2:20–21). Therefore, the Lord left those nations without driving them out hastily nor delivering them into the hand of Joshua.

In the sixth cycle of disobedience to God, He led them into forty years of oppression at the hands of the Philistines. Then God used Samson to save the Israelites from the Philistines, but not before his leadership was marked by moral and spiritual failure as much as it was by military success.

Samson was born from a barren woman, and the angel of the Lord appeared unto the woman. She would conceive and bear a son, but he should not cut the hair on his head, for the child should be a Nazarite to God from the womb, and he should deliver Israel out of the hand of the Philistines.

To help him accomplish God's plan, he received enormous physical strength through his long hair. He was in numerous scrapes, wasting his strength on practical jokes that he eventually gave up altogether to satisfy the woman he loved. His wife's name was Delilah. Samson lied to her about where his strength came from many times. She continued to press him daily to reveal his strength. Finally, Samson told her that he had been a Nazarite to God from his mother's womb, "If I shave, then my strength will go from me, and I shall become weak and like any other man" (Judges 16:17). Then Delilah called the lords of the Philistines, telling them to come up at once. Then the lords of the Philistines came to her and brought money. Delilah made Samson sleep upon her knees, and she called for a man to shave off the seven locks of his head, and his strength went from him.

Delilah told Samson the Philistines were upon him, so he awoke out of his sleep and said, "I will go out same as other times and shake myself free" (Judges 16:20). He did not seem to care that the Lord was departed from him. But the Philistines took him, put out his eyes, brought him down to Gaza, bound him with fetters of brass, and he did grind in the prison house. His hair did begin to grow again after he was shaven.

The lords of the Philistines, when their hearts were merry, called for Samson so they could make him a sport for them. Samson did make himself a sport to them, and they set him between the pillars. Samson said unto the lad who held his hand to let him feel the pillars so that he could lean upon them. The house was full of men and women, and all the lords of the Philistines were there, and there were about three thousand men and women who would watch the sport. Samson called to the Lord to strengthen him so that he could avenge the Philistines. He bowed himself with all his might, and the house fell upon the lords and upon all the people who were there. The dead he slew, including himself, were more than he had killed in his life.

Ruth, the Moab, was one of the few people who loved God and served as a bright shining light in the midst of the darkness in this period of history. There was a famine in Bethlehem-Judah, so Naomi's husband, Elimelech, took her and their two sons to the country of Moab. They dwelled there for about ten years. Naomi's husband and two sons died.

Naomi decided to return to her country, and Ruth, her daughter-in-law, insisted that she go to Bethlehem with her. God showed Himself faithful by providing Boaz, Elimelech's rich relative, to keep the family line intact. Ruth became his wife. Boaz treated Ruth with compassion when she and Naomi needed food. Boaz and Ruth had a son who would be the grandfather of David—Israel's greatest king. Boaz begot Obed, and Obed begot Jesse, and Jesse begot David.

Israel was ruled by judges for three hundred years, and Samuel was the last of those judges. Samuel was a special child, a gift from

God to a barren woman who gave him to God to grow up in the tabernacle as a priest in training under Eli and could qualify to serve Israel as both a priest and judge. The nations had fallen away from God, but God was preparing Samuel to lead the nations back to the right living. God is always in control and can bring His people back to Him.

Eli was an excellent priest, but he was a poor parent. His sons brought him grief and ruin. The two things he lacked were firm discipline and action. God pointed out his sons' errors. Both love and discipline must be spoken and acted out. Eli had another problem of feeling he had to protect the symbols. A relic or antique needs to be stored away safely; God's Word must be used and obeyed.

The Philistines continued to plague the Israelites, and the poor leadership in Israel continued to show itself as the sons of Eli brought the ark into battle, only to have it captured by the enemy. A man came into Shilou and told that the ark had been taken by the Philistines and all the city cried out. When Eli, now ninety-eight years old, his eyes so dim, he could not see, asked the man, "What is there done, my son?" he told Eli that he had fled before the Philistines, and there had been a great slaughter among the people of Israel, and his two sons also were slain, and the ark of God was taken. When Eli heard what had happened to the ark of God, he fell off the seat backward, broke his neck, and died. He was old, heavy in stature, and he had judged Israel for forty years. God brought the ark safely home to Israel, and He used Samuel to subdue the Philistines and restore peace to Israel.

The Israelites wanted to be like "all the other nations" who had a king to fight their battles. They conveniently forgot that it was their faithfulness that brought them under attack in the first place. Their rebellion served to carry out God's purpose of having a kingdom in Israel over which Jesus, the Messiah, would someday reign. The Lord accordingly authorized Samuel to anoint a king and directed him to Saul.

Saul's accession went ahead in three steps: he was anointed by Samuel and filled with God's Spirit, then publicly selected at Mizpah, and last, popularly selected at Mizpah. The primary concern of his forty-year reign was the Philistines. They had occupied much of his territory. Then an open war was provoked when one of their garrisons was destroyed by Saul's son Jonathan. His personal bravery, plus the Philistines' open superstitious reaction to a heaven-sent earthquake, brought about their total defeat. Saul's failure to give in to Samuel made him suffer the rejection of his dynasty from the throne of Israel.

Samuel then privately anointed David, a son of Jesse of Judah, as king over Israel. David was about fifteen at the time, but by God's providence, he gained rapid promotion at court—first as a minstrel and then by his victory over the Philistine giant Goliath. Saul's jealousy drove David and his followers into exile. Saul diverted his resources in a futile pursuit of David. The Philistines prepared for a third all-out attack on Israel. Saul was routed at Mount Gilboa and committed suicide rather than suffer capture.

David wanted to construct a temple in Jerusalem that would be fitting for the Lord, but because David had excessive bloodshed, he was denied by God. David also had some major personal and family problems, but his repentance, dependence on God, and responsiveness to God's prophets demonstrated the kind of faith God wanted in the leader of His people. But God's prophet informed David that the Lord Himself would build a house. God would raise up David's offspring, Solomon, to succeed David, and he would be the one to build a house for God. Israel's ultimate purpose would be fulfilled.

"And I will establish the throne of His kingdom forever. I will be His (the Messiah's) Father and He will be My Son" (2 Samuel 13:14). The eternal Christ would rise in power to give death to sin and then later would rise in power to give everlasting life to His own. In the Lord's promise to him, David experienced fundamental clarification of God's former redemptive revelation on Mount Sinai, so when David was aged, he made his son, Solomon, king over Israel. David said, "The Lord God of Israel has given rest to His people, that they may dwell in Jerusalem forever" (1 Chronicles 23:25).

David told Solomon, "Be strong and of good courage, and build the house of the Lord; do not fear nor be dismayed, for the Lord God will be with you. He will not forsake you" (1 Chronicles 28:20). Solomon asked God for wisdom and knowledge so that he may guide God's people. God granted his wish and included riches, wealth, and honor. Solomon was determined to build a temple in the name of the Lord and a royal house for himself. The ark was to be put in the house of the Lord and included with the ark the covenant of the Lord, which He made with the children of Israel.

But Solomon did not follow God with his whole heart as his father had. He married many foreign women and added worship of their gods to his halfhearted worship of the true God. This set the tragic division of the nations after his death, set disobedience and idolatry that Israel struggled with for generations.

God wants His people to be wise. Two kinds of people portray two contrasting paths in life: the fool (the wicked and stubborn person who hates or ignores God) and the wise person (who seeks to know and love God). When we choose God's way, He will grant us wisdom. His Word and the Bible lead us to live right, have the right relationships, and make the right decisions. Praise to God is recognizing, appreciating, and experiencing God's greatness. Focusing our thoughts on God moves us to praise Him. The more we know Him, the more we can appreciate what He has done for us and what He continues to do for us and through us.

After Solomon died, his son Rehoboam continued imposing heavy taxes and labor on the people, and they revolted against him. Ten of the twelve tribes united under Jeroboam, who was Solomon's servant. He received ten tribes; Solomon had one tribe for the sake of his father, David, and for the sake of Jerusalem, which God had chosen out of all the tribes of Israel. And the period that Solomon reigned in Jerusalem over all of Israel was forty years. There was war between Rehoboam and Jeroboam all their days. From then on, there were many kings.

Even Elijah's love for God could not turn the Israelites back to God; while they were in the land, they were scattered among two large tribes. God raised up the Assyrians to conquer Israel, scatter the Israelites throughout the world, and repopulate the land with exiles from other conquered nations.

God spared the southern nation of Judah from Assyria, using the prophets Isaiah and Micah along with The Good King Hezekiah to lead the nation back to Him temporarily, but the reforms would not last. Judah always went back to worshipping idols, rejecting God and His prophets, wanting to be like the nations around them, and so God brought the powerful Babylonian Empire against them in judgment.

Daniel and Ezekiel began their ministries during this period. They were a shining light for the people of God in this bleak and dark time.

PROPHETS

Jonah was a reluctant prophet given a mission he found distasteful. He chose to run away from God rather than obey Him. Instead of going to preach to the wicked people in Nineveh, he took a ship in the opposite direction. He was afraid they would hear his message, that they would repent, and that God would forgive the city that had for many years grievously oppressed his own land. During a violent storm at sea, the heathen sailors prayed to their own gods to see who had offended them and caused this storm. Jonah volunteered to be thrown overboard for their sakes. This was done, the storm subsided, and the sailors offered a sacrifice to God.

The Lord prepared a great fish to swallow Jonah. Surprised to find himself alive in the belly of the fish, the prophet gave thanks to God and expressed the confident hope that he would be delivered. After three days and three nights, the fish vomited him onto the dry land. The people of Nineveh repented in sackcloth and ashes, and God spared the city. God gave Jonah a second chance to go to Nineveh, and this time Jonah didn't run. He went to Nineveh, but when the people responded to his announcement of God's judgment by repenting, Jonah became angry that God did not destroy the city as He had threatened. Jonah was a prophet who didn't want to see the people respond; he simply wanted God to destroy people he considered to be enemies. Do you ever find yourself upset at the mercy God shows to others? If so, perhaps consider God's response to Jonah and rethink your anger.

Like Jonah, we may have to do things in life that we don't want to do. Sometimes we find ourselves wanting to turn and run. But it is better to obey God than to defy Him and run away. Often, despite our defiance, God, in His mercy, will give us another chance to serve Him.

Isaiah was the first prophet of the southern kingdom of Judah and one of four major prophets. He has been called the "Prince of Prophets." Isaiah was a native of Jerusalem in the southern kingdom of Judah. His ministry was about sixty years of service. Isaiah's call was a dramatic experience—a vision of the holiness and purity of God. He saw his own worthiness. He confessed his sins, received cleansing from the Lord, and made himself available to God. God gave him the commission to go to sinful, needy people with a message of warning and judgment but also with the good news of forgiveness and deliverance. God was about to abandon Judah until Isaiah preached to the people. By this treatment, God meant to lead His people to repentance and righteousness. The Lord is far more concerned about the purity of His people than how rich they are. Isaiah called on his people to repent and turn back to God. He has been called the evangelist of the Old Testament. Many of the most precious verses in the Bible came to us from his lips. The fact that Jesus began His public ministry at the age of thirty in Nazareth by reading from Isaiah and applying his prophetic words to Himself is significant to the place that this book would come to hold in the Christian church. As a foreteller, Isaiah told how God's ultimate plan would finally triumph through His preserving a remnant of His people and through the suffering and death of His appointed Servant, the Lord Jesus Christ.

Jeremiah was a prophet who endured. He had to depend on God's love as he endured the race ahead of him. Usually, his audiences were antagonistic. He was ignored; his life was ignored; his life was often threatened. He saw both the excitement of spiritual awakening and the sorrow of a natural return to idolatry. Most of the kings ignored his warnings and led the people away from God. He saw fellow prophets murdered. Jeremiah himself was severely persecuted. Finally, he watched Judah's defeat at the hands of the Babylonians. Jeremiah would feel tempted to give up, but he knew he had to keep going. God had called him to endure. He was very tense and saw the feelings of God, who was soon to execute justice and who afterward would show mercy. God may reprimand us, but He always comes back with love and mercy for us.

Babylon came back a second time and took another larger group of people from Judah into exile, including King Jehoiachin and his prophet Ezekiel. The Babylonians set up their own king, who was the uncle of Jehoiachin. They changed his name to Zedekiah to show further dominance over Judah. The prophet Ezekiel declared the certainty of impending judgment on Jerusalem. God's people had broken the terms of the Lord's covenant with them at Mount Sinai and now faced the curses of death and destruction that were attached to the covenant. Only after these curses had taken effect could there be any hope for the future.

In 586 BC, Judah's expulsion from the land of Judah was completed by Babylon. They seized Jerusalem, sacked the city, and destroyed the temple and walls. All but the poorest and weakest people of Judah were either killed or carried off to exile. God's promises of judgment for Judah's sins were fulfilled, but God continued to speak to His people through the prophets and in prayer and even His judgment on sin.

God is always faithful to His promises. The land was laid to waste, and it looked like God had abandoned His people. Even the temple, which was designed as the center for the proper worship of God and meant to be a light to the nations, had been destroyed by the Babylonian armies of the Babylon Empire. Almost all the people had been killed or exiled to Babylon. The northern territory had been wiped out and scattered by Assyria. More than a century earlier, when the people left Judah, they asked Jeremiah what they should do with themselves. He prayed to God and then advised them to remain in the Promised Land and trust God to preserve and protect them. Jeremiah informed the people they could rely on God rather than flee to Egypt. But the people left, ignored the message of the prophet, and went to Egypt, where they died.

Daniel was a highly placed government official in both Babylon and Persia, but his heart was always with his people and his God. One day, he was reading from the prophecies of Jeremiah and realized that the seventy years of exile were about to end. His prayer of repentance for the sins of his people and his request for God to restore them to the land were the climax of the exile. Now, would God respond and restore His people? Nebuchadnezzar was the greatest of the Babylonian kings. He thought of himself as a god. God used him for His own purposes. Nebuchadnezzar thought he could get more cooperation if the people he conquered could worship their own gods. He did take their lands, their riches he robbed, their lives he controlled, but their idols he allowed them to worship and even sometimes to worship them himself. He was very prideful. When he conquered the little nation of Judah, he met God, who demanded exclusive worship, not just His share among many gods. Nebuchadnezzar had always been able to rule the gods, but God dared to claim that He had made Nebuchadnezzar all that he was. God allowed him victories. He allowed him to deport the best young Jewish leaders as his palace servants, including placing

Daniel there, who would change the king's life. God allowed Nebuchadnezzar to attempt to kill three of his servants to teach the king that he did not really have power over life and death. God warned him of the dangers in his pride and then allowed Nebuchadnezzar to live through seven years of insanity before restoring him to the throne. God showed the king who was really in control.

The prophets console the people by telling them that the day will come when God will be their king and shepherd. He will give His people a new heart to worship Him, and He will reestablish His presence among them through a new temple.

We must be faithful to God because we love Him and not just for what He can do for us. We should give glory every day, for creation, for Jesus, for the Holy Spirit, for creating us and caring for us in our mothers' wombs, and for supplying a purpose for our lives. God is all-knowing: He takes charge of world events; God overrules and removes rebellious leaders who defy Him. God will overcome evil; no one is exempt. But He will deliver the faithful who follow Him. Nations sin for world control now; one day, Christ's kingdom will replace and surpass the kingdoms of this world. Our faith is sure because our future is secure in Christ. We must have courage and put our faith in God, who controls everything.

God's people lived in exile for two generations. But then the Persian Empire swept through the entire region and conquered Judah's captors, the Babylonians. Persia had a policy of allowing people to return to their homelands and resume their own customs and religions, so God's people returned to Jerusalem and began to restore their nation.

The largest group under the leadership of Zerubbabel settled in the land around Jerusalem to work on the temple. It took twenty years to complete because they faced opposition from the people who had been living in and near Jerusalem. The second group consisted of about 2,000 families and the Scribe and Priest Ezra. When they arrived, the temple was nearly completed, but the people's spiritual lives were in ruin. The Israelites had intermarried with the people from surrounding nations and had begun to follow their gods instead of remaining faithful to the Lord. Ezra confronted them with their sin and called them to repentance and renewal.

Nehemiah came with a small group of people to encourage the rebuilding of Jerusalem's wall. Despite the strong opposition from the people around Jerusalem, Nehemiah successfully led the Jews in rebuilding the wall around Jerusalem and securing the city for God's people. Nehemiah confronted the people with their sins and called on them to repent and return to the Lord.

Joel and Malachi, prophets, came after Nehemiah to challenge the people on their sinfulness and encourage them to remain faithful to the Lord while they awaited His final salvation.

Many Jewish people remained in the cities where God had placed them throughout the Persian Empire. There, Esther, a Jewish orphan, was raised by her uncle Mordecai and became Queen of Persia after the king's wife refused to obey his command. God put Esther in this position to save her people from Haman, the king's chief minister.

Mordecai refused to bow down, so Haman wanted him killed, but Esther told the king about Haman's scheme to destroy her people. The king became angry and ordered Haman to be hung on the gallows that he had planned for Mordecai's death. The king had sent out another decree that enabled the Jews to save themselves.

NEW TESTAMENT

It was during the Roman Era that the Israelites could offer little resistance. Pompey sacked Jerusalem in 63 BC, so the Jews were once again under the command of a foreign ruler. Herod the Great became king of the Jews, and it was under his rule that Jesus was born, ushering in a new era in biblical history.

Israel had been waiting for their Messiah, and there were many expectations about what He would do for them and how it would look. They recalled the glory of the age of David and Solomon. The Messiah was expected to be the climax of Israel's story, the ultimate fulfillment of all God's promises to His people. Nobody expected the Messiah to come as the baby of a humble peasant girl from a small, unimportant town in Galilee.

But Jesus is the climax of God's story! He is the ultimate fulfillment of all God's promises to His people! The four Gospels, Matthew, Mark, John, and Luke, tell the story of how this man from the margins of Israel's society displayed God's power through mighty miracles and through teaching with authority. They tell the story of how this unlikely Messiah gave the world far more than any military or political or religious leader ever could have. They tell the story of "God with us," the eternal Son of God made flesh to live among His people and offer them salvation and eternal life. This was far more than the meager kingdoms they were hoping for.

"The Holy Spirit will come upon you, and the power of the Highest will overshadow you; therefore, also, that Holy One who is born will be called the Son of God" (Luke 1:35). He was one of the Triune, which included God, Jesus, and the Holy Spirit all in one. The King of Israel, the Servant Savior, the God of the Universe, was born as a humble infant, grew up in the small village of Nazareth, and began His ministry by submitting to the baptism of John.

"In the beginning was the Word and the Word was with God, and the Word was God" (John 1:1). He was at the beginning with God. There was a man sent from God whose name was John. In the days of Herod, king of Judah, a priest named Zacharias and his wife Elisabeth were both righteous with God; they were blameless with God; they were blameless in the Ten Commandments, all the ordinances of the Lord. Elisabeth was barren, and she and her husband were well into their later years. As an angel of the Lord appeared before Zacharias, he was troubled and fearful. The angel told him to fear not, for his prayer was being answered, and Elisabeth would give birth to a son. He was great in the sight of the Lord and was filled with the Holy Spirit, even before he was born. Many people would rejoice at his birth. Many children of Israel were turned to the Lord their God. God chose John to go before Jesus in the Spirit and power of Elias so he could turn the hearts of the fathers to the children and the disobedient to the wisdom of the just; to make ready a people prepared for the Lord.

Zacharias wanted to know how he would know these things. God sent His angel Gabriel to show him these glad tidings. And as it happened, Zacharias became mute, not able to speak until the day that these things would be performed because he believed not in words spoken for their season. After Zacharias finished his ministry, he went home to Elisabeth. After that, Elisabeth conceived, and she hid for five months.

Then in the sixth month of Elisabeth's pregnancy, the angel Gabriel was sent by God to Nazareth to a virgin who was to be married to a man whose name was Joseph. Her name was Mary. The angel came to Mary and said, "Hail thou that art highly favored, the Lord is with thee: blessed art though among women" (Luke 1:28).

The angel of the Lord appeared to Joseph, saying, "Joseph, son of David, do not be afraid to take to you Mary as your wife, because conceived in her is of the Holy Spirit. And she will bring forth a Son, and you shall call His name Jesus for He will save His people from their sins" (Matthew 1:20–21). Spoken by the Lord through the prophet saying, "'Behold the virgin shall be with child, and bear a Son, and they shall call His name Immanuel,' which is translated, 'God with us'" (Matthew 1:23).

Mary wanted to know how this could be because she was a virgin. The angel answered and said the power of the Holy Spirit would come upon her and the power of the Highest would overshadow; therefore, also, the Holy One who was to be born would be called the Son of God. Mary was told that her cousin, Elisabeth, was in her sixth month of pregnancy even though she had been barren. "For with God nothing will be impossible" (Luke 1:37). Mary left quickly to the City of Judah, where Zacharias and Elisabeth greeted her, and she stayed three months. Then she returned to her house. John, Elisabeth's child, grew and became strong in Spirit and stayed in the desert until the day of his manifestation to Israel.

A decree went out from Caesar Augustus that all the world should be registered; they all went to their own cities. Joseph was out of the lineage of David, and he had to go to Bethlehem to be registered with Mary, his betrothed wife who was with child. Mary gave birth to her firstborn Son, Jesus; she wrapped Him in swaddling clothes and laid Him in a manger because there was no room at the inn.

There were some shepherds living out in the country, and they were in fear as an angel of the Lord approached them and as the glory of God shone around them. The angel told them not to fear because he was bringing them good tidings of great joy, which would be to all people. There was born a Savior in the city of David, who was Christ the Lord. The shepherds went to the city to find out what it was all about. After eight days passed, the child, whose name was Jesus, was circumcised because this was the law of God that had to be performed. After Mary's purification from the birth of Jesus, they returned to Jerusalem.

There was a man in Jerusalem whose name was Simon who was very righteous and devout. He was waiting for the consolation of Israel. The Holy Spirit was upon him and told him he should not see death before he had seen the Lord's Christ. He entered the temple. When he saw Mary and Joseph with Jesus, he took Jesus out of their arms and blessed God and said, "Lord, now You are letting Your servant die in peace. According to Your word; for mine eyes have seen Your salvation that You preferred before the face of all people. A light to lighten the Gentiles and the glory of Your people Israel" (Luke 2:29–32).

Wise men came from the east to Jerusalem, wanting to know that Jesus was born King of the Jews. King Herod and all of Jerusalem were troubled when they heard about Jesus. He demanded the whereabouts of Jesus from all the chief priests and scribes of the people. Herod sent the wise men to find Jesus so he could go and worship Him, too. When the wise men found Jesus, they presented their gifts, gold, frankincense, and myrrh. God warned them in a dream that they should not return to Herod, and they departed back to their own country another way.

The angel of the Lord warned Joseph, in a dream, to take his family into Egypt and to stay there until God told them otherwise because Herod was looking to destroy Jesus. So they stayed in Egypt until Herod's death. God told them to return to Israel, but when they found out Herod's son was the ruler, they turned aside into the parts of Galilee, and they came to live in Nazareth. There Jesus grew, became strong in Spirit, filled with wisdom, and the grace of God was on Him.

Every year His parents went to Jerusalem for the feast of Passover. When Jesus was twelve years old, after the feast, Mary and Joseph went on home, not realizing that Jesus had stayed behind, so when they realized, they returned to Jerusalem. After three days, they found Him in the temple sitting with doctors, both hearing and asking them questions. They were astonished by His understanding and answers. Jesus asked His parents why they were looking for Him because He was doing His Father's business. Jesus went back home with them and increased in wisdom and stature and in favor with God and man.

In the Judean wilderness, John the Baptist, dressed in camel hair with a leather belt around his waist and eating locust and honey, was preaching to people to repent, "for the kingdom of heaven is at hand" (Matthew 4:17). After hearing this, Jerusalem, all of Judea, and all the regions around the Jordan came out so he could baptize them in the river, confessing their sins. John told them that he baptized by water, but He who was coming after him was mightier than him, whose sandals he could not be worthy to carry. He would baptize with the Holy Spirit and fire.

Jesus left Galilee to go to John at the Jordan River to be baptized. John tried to stop Jesus from baptizing Him first, but Jesus said to him, "Permit it to be so now, for this is fitting for us to fulfill all righteousness" (Matthew 3:15). Then John allowed Jesus to be baptized first. When He came up from the water, as the heavens were opening to Him, He saw the Spirit of God descending like a dove and alighting on Him. Suddenly the voice of God from heaven said, "This is My Beloved Son, in whom I am well pleased" (Matthew 3:17).

Immediately Jesus was driven to the wilderness by the Holy Spirit to spend forty days and forty nights tempted by Satan, and He was with beasts. During that time, the angels ministered to Him. When Jesus was hungry, Satan said to Him, "If you are really the Son of God, command these stones to be made into bread" (Matthew 4:3). Jesus told Satan, "It is written, man shall not live by bread alone, but by every word that proceeded out of the mouth of God" (Matthew 4:4). Because Jesus didn't turn the stones into bread, Satan took Him into the holy city, sat Him on a pinnacle of the temple, and said to

Him that if He was the Son of God, to cast Himself down. For it is written: "He shall give His angels charge concerning Him," and, "In their hands, they shall bear Him up, lest at any time you dash your foot against a stone" (Matthew 4:6). Jesus said to Satan, "It is written again; you shall not tempt the Lord your God" (Matthew 4:7). Then after that, Satan took Him up to a very high mountain, showed Him all the kingdom of the world and the glory of them, and said to Him, "All these things I will give to You if You fall and worship me" (Matthew 4:9). Then Jesus said to him, "Get thee behind Me Satan! For it is written: you shall worship the Lord your God, and Him only shall you serve" (Matthew 4:10). Then Satan left, and the angels went and ministered to Him.

Three days later, Jesus' mother was invited to a marriage in Cana of Galilee. Jesus and His disciples went to the marriage, and when they wanted wine, the mother of Jesus told them that there wasn't any left. Jesus asked His mother, "What has this to do with Me?" His mother said to the servants, "Whatsoever He says unto you, do it" (John 2:5). There sat six waterpots, each seven-eighth of a gallon, Jesus told them to fill the waterpots with water, and they filled them to the brim. He told them not to drink from the pots but give it to the governor of the feast. Every man at the beginning of the feast always gets the best wine. When the bridegroom tasted the wine, it was better than his best, and this turned out to be the first miracle that Jesus performed with people. The disciples believed in Him. Then Jesus, His mother, His brethren, and the disciples went down to Capernaum and continued from there.

Now John was put in prison, and Jesus came to Galilee preaching the gospel of the king. He said, "The time is at hand. Repent and believe in the gospel" (Mark 1:15). As He walked by the Sea of Galilee, He saw Simon and his brother Andrew casting a net into the sea because they were fishermen. Jesus said to them, "Follow Me, and I will make you become fishers of men" (Matthew 4:19). Immediately, they followed Him. A little farther, Jesus saw James and John, sons of Zebedee, who were in the boat taking care of their nets. Jesus called to James and John; they left immediately to follow. Their father stayed with the servants.

When they reached Capernaum on the Sabbath, He immediately went into the synagogue to teach. They were amazed how Jesus spoke in authority and not as a scribe. While they were in the synagogue, a man with an unclean spirit was calling out to have Jesus leave him alone. What did He have to do with them? They thought He had come to destroy them. The unclean man told Him he knew Jesus was the Holy One of God. "But Jesus rebuked him, saying, 'Be quiet, and come out of him!'" (Mark 1:25). The unclean spirit convulsed him, cried out with a loud voice, and the unclean spirit came out of his body. They were all amazed that Jesus commanded with authority that even the unclean spirits obeyed Him. Jesus' fame spread throughout all the region around Galilee.

As soon as they left the synagogue, they went to the house of Simon and Andrew with James and John. But Simon's mother-in-law was sick with fever, and they told Him about her at once. Jesus took her by the hand, lifted her up, and immediately, the fever was gone.

And she served them. When the sun set, they brought Jesus to all who were sick and those who were demon-possessed. The whole city was gathered by her door, and Jesus healed many who were sick with various diseases and cast out many demons to speak because they knew Him.

When He had come to the other side, to Gergesenes, He was met with two demon-possessed men, coming out of the tombs, exceedingly fierce, so that no one could pass that way. And suddenly, they cried out, saying, "What have we to do with You, Jesus, Son of God? Have You come here to torment us before the time?" (Matthew 8:29). Now, there was a herd of many swine feeding a long way off from them, so the demons begged Him, saying, "If You cast us out, permit us to go away into the herd of the swine" (Matthew 8:31). And Jesus said to them, "Go." When the demons came out of their bodies, they went into the herd of swine, and suddenly all the swine ran violently down the steep place into the sea and perished in the water. The people who fed the swine left and went into the city and told everything, including what had happened to the demon-possessed men. And behold, the whole city came out to meet Jesus. And when they saw Jesus, they begged Him to depart from the region (Matthew 8:28–34).

Jesus rose before daylight and departed to a solitary place to pray. When Simon and those who were with him were searching for Jesus, and they found Him, they told Him they were looking for Him, but Jesus said, "Let us go to the next towns that I may preach there; also, because this is My purpose I have come forth" (Mark 1:38). Then

Jesus preached through Galilee in the synagogues casting out demons. A leper came to Him and knelt, saying, "If you are willing, You can make me clean" (Matthew 8:2). Jesus moved with compassion, stretching out His hand and touching him, saying, "I am willing; be cleansed" (Matthew 8:3). The leper was healed as Jesus spoke. After listening to Jesus, all in the synagogue were filled with wrath; they rose and thrust Him out of the city; they led Him to the brow of the hill on which their city was built that they might throw Him down over the cliff. Then He pressed through the midst of them and went on His way.

As the multitudes pressed about Him to hear the Word of God, He stood by the lake of Gergesenes. He saw two boats, but the fishermen were with the boats because they were washing their nets. Then Jesus got in one of the boats, which was Simon's, and asked him to put out a little from the land. And He sat down and taught the multitudes from the boat. After speaking, Jesus asked Simon, "Launch out into the deep and let down your nets for a catch" (Luke 5:4). Simon told Jesus, "Master, I have worked all night and caught nothing, but I at Your word I will let down the nets" (Luke 5:5). When they let down their nets, as Jesus said, they caught an over-abundance of fish, and their nets were breaking. They signaled for their partners in the other boat to come and help them. They filled both boats and began to sink. When Simon Peter saw it, he knelt at Jesus' knees, saying, "Depart from me, for I am a sinful man, O Lord!" (Luke 5:8). They were all astonished at the number of fish they caught. Jesus said to Simon, "Do not be afraid. From now on you will catch men" (Luke 5:10). They brought their boats to land and followed Him. Then Jesus withdrew into the wilderness to pray.

On a certain day, as He was teaching, there were Pharisees and teachers of the law of Moses sitting by who had come out of every town of Galilee, Judea, and Jerusalem. And the power of the Lord was present to heal them. Men brought a paralyzed man whom they sought to bring in and lay before Jesus. There was such a large crowd they could not find how they might bring him in, so they went up on the roof. They let him down with his bed through the tiling into the midst before Jesus. When Jesus saw their faith, He said to him, "Man, your sins are forgiven you" (Luke 5:20). The Pharisees and scribes began to reason, saying, "Who is this that speaks blasphemies? Who can forgive sins but God alone?" (Luke 5:21). Jesus answered them and said, "Why are you reasoning in your hearts? Which is easier to say, 'Your sins are forgiven you, or to say, 'Rise up and walk'? But that you may know that the Son of Man has power on earth to forgive sins." He said to the man who was paralyzed, "I say to you, arise, take up your bed, and go to your house." Immediately he rose, took up what he had been laying on, and departed to his own house, glorifying God. And they were all amazed, and they glorified God and were filled with fear, saying, "We have seen strange things today!" (Luke 5:22–26).

The Jewish Passover feast was at hand, so Jesus and His disciples went to Jerusalem. There He found those who were selling oxen, sheep, doves, and money changers doing business. After making a whip of cords, He drove all out of the temple and overturned the tables. The

Jews asked for a sign to be shown to them since He did these things; Jesus answered and said to them, "Destroy this temple, and in three days I will raise it up." (He was referring to His resurrection.) The Jews told Him it had taken forty-six years to build, so how could He raise it in three days? But He was speaking of the temple of His body. Now when Jesus was in Jerusalem at the Passover, during the feast, many believed in His name when they saw miracles that He did. Because Jesus knew what was in man, He did not commit Himself.

A man of the Pharisees named Nicodemus, a ruler of the Jews, said to Him, "Rabbi, we know that You are a teacher come from God: for no one can do these signs that you do unless God is with Him" (John 3:2). Jesus answered and said to him, "Most assuredly, I say to you, unless one is born again, he cannot see the kingdom of God." (John 3:3). No matter how intelligent and well-educated you are, you must come to Jesus with an open mind and heart so He can teach you the truth about God. Nicodemus knew from the Bible the kingdom would be ruled by God, it would be restored on earth, and it would incorporate God's people. Jesus told Nicodemus the kingdom would come to the whole world (John 3:16), not just for the Jews, and that Nicodemus wouldn't be part of it unless he was personally born again (John 3:5). The entrance requirements are repentance and spiritual rebirth. Jesus later taught that God's kingdom has already begun in the hearts of believers (Luke 17:21). It will be fully realized when Jesus returns, again, to judge the world and abolish evil forever (Revelation 21:22). The Pharisees had heard that Jesus made and baptized more disciples than John (though Jesus Himself did not baptize, His disciples did). Since Jesus did not baptize, He left Judea and departed to Galilee, but He needed to go through Samaria.

Jesus came to Sychar, the City of Samaria, which was near a plot of ground given to Joseph by his father Jacob, which had a well. He was weary from His journey. A woman of Samaria came to draw water, and Jesus said to her, "Give Me a drink." His disciples had gone to the city to buy food. The Samarian woman said to Him, "How is it that you, a Jew, ask a drink from me as a Samarian woman?" for Jews had no dealings with Samarians. Jesus answered and said to her, "If you knew the gift of God, and who says to you, 'Give me a drink,' you would have asked Him, and He would have given you living water." The woman wanted to know where Jesus got that living water. She said, "Are you greater than our father Jacob, who gave us the well and drank from it himself, as well as his sons and his livestock?" (John 4:12). Jesus answered and said to her, "Whoever drinks of this water will thirst again, but whoever drinks of this water that I shall give him will never thirst. But the water that I shall give him will become in him a fountain of water springing up into everlasting life." The woman said to Him, "Sir, give me this water that I may not thirst nor come here to drink." Jesus said to her, "Go call your husband and come here." The woman answered, "I have no husband." Jesus said to her, "You have well said, 'I have no husband.' For you have had five husbands, and the one whom you now have is not your husband; in that, you spoke truly." The woman said to Him, "Sir, I perceive that You are a prophet" (John 4:12).

"Our fathers worship on this mountain, and you Jews say that Jerusalem is the place where one ought to worship." Jesus said to her,

"Woman, believe Me, the hour is coming when you will neither on this mountain nor in Jerusalem worship the Father. You worship what you do not know; we know what we worship for salvation is of the Jews. But the hour is coming, and now is when the true worshippers will worship the Father in Spirit and truth; for the Father is seeking such to worship Him must worship in Spirit and truth." The woman said to Him, "I know that my Messiah is coming" (who is called Christ). "When He comes, He will tell us all things." Jesus said to her, "I who speak to you am He" (John 4:20–26).

About this time, the disciples returned; and they marveled that Jesus was talking to the woman, but no one asked why. The woman left her waterpot and went into the city and told the men, "Come see a man who told me all things that I ever did. Could this be the Christ?" Then they went out of the city and came to Jesus. The disciples urged Him to eat, but Jesus said to them, "My food is to do the will of Him who sent Me and to finish His work. Do you not say, 'There are still four months and then the harvest'? Behold, I say to you, open your eyes and look at the fields, for they are already white for the harvest! And he who reaps may rejoice together. For in this, the saying is true: 'One sows and another reaps. I sent you to reap that for which you have not labored; others have labored, and you have entered into their labors.'" And many of the Samaritans believed in Him because of the word of the woman who testified, "He told me all that I ever did" (John 4:27–39).

The Samaritans urged Him to stay with them, and He stayed two days. Many more believed because of His own word. After listening to Jesus, they knew from what He said that He was Christ, the Savior of the world. After two days, He went to Galilee (John 4:40–43).

Jesus went to Cana of Galilee again, and there was a certain nobleman whose son was dying. He went to Jesus and implored Him to come and heal his son. Jesus said to him, "Unless your people see signs and wonders, you will by no means believe." The nobleman said to Him, "Sir, come down before my child dies!" Jesus said to him, "Go your way; your son lives." The man believed and was going home when he ran into his servants. They told him his son lived. The servants told him the fever left his son on the seventh hour, so he knew from this that the hour of healing by Jesus was at the same time (John 4:46–53).

After this, there was a feast of the Jews, and Jesus went up to Jerusalem. There was a pool by the Sheep Gate called Bethesda, and there were five porches. There lay sick people, blind, lame, paralyzed, waiting for the moving of the water. An angel went down at a certain time to stir the water, and whoever stepped in first was healed of whatever disease he had. A certain man who had an infirmity for thirty-eight years was approached by Jesus. Jesus said to him, "Do you want to be made well?" The man wanted to be healed, but he had no one to put him in the pool while the water was stirred. Jesus said to him, "Rise, take up your bed and walk." Immediately he was healed and did what Jesus said. The Jews said to the man who was cured, "It is the Sabbath; it is not lawful for you to carry your bed." He said to them, "He who made me well said to me, 'Take up your bed and walk.'" Then the Jews asked who the man was, who said to take your bed and walk? Jesus left and was found in the temple with multitudes, but He told the man, "See, you have been made well. Sin no more, lest a worse thing come upon you." The man departed and told the Jews it was Jesus who had made him well. For this reason, the Jews persecuted Jesus and sought to kill Him because He had done these things on the Sabbath. But Jesus answered them, "My Father has been working until now, and I have been working" (John 5:1–17).

Jesus cannot do of Himself, but only what His Father does in like manner. God shows the Son of Man all things and would show Him greater works so that they may marvel. God raises the dead and gives life to them; even so, the Son gives life to whom He will. The Father does not judge, but He has committed all judgment to Jesus. If you do not honor Jesus, you do not honor the Father who sent Him. "If you hear My word and believe in Him who sent Me, you will have everlasting life and shall not come into judgment but pass from death into life" (John 5:24).

The hour is coming when we as the deaf will hear the voice of the Son of God, and those who hear will live. The Son has life in Himself just as the Father has life in Himself and has given Him authority to execute judgment also because He is the Son of Man. Do not marvel at this, for those in the graves will hear His voice and come forth. Those who have done good, to the resurrection of life; those who have done evil, to the resurrection of condemnation. Jesus said He could do nothing. "As I hear, I judge; and My judgment is righteous because I do not seek My own will but the will of the Father who sent Me"

(John 5:25–30). In your prayers to Jesus, state whatever you want to do or receive; let it be done according to God's will. All prayers are through Jesus because He is the advocate of God. We are all sinners, so after praying, say you ask everything in the name of Jesus.

On the second Sabbath, Jesus and His disciples went through the corn field, and His disciples began to pluck the ears of corn. The Pharisees asked Jesus why they did that because working on the Sabbath was unlawful. Jesus told them the Sabbath was made for man and not man for the Sabbath: the Son of Man is Lord also of the Sabbath (Mark 2:23–28).

After Jesus departed, He went into their synagogue and found a man with a withered hand, and they asked Him, "Is it lawful to heal on the Sabbath day?" so that they might be able to accuse Him. Then Jesus said to them that if one sheep fell in the pit, would they not go to the sheep and lift it out? How much then is a man better than a sheep? Then Jesus told the man, "Stretch forth your hand." And he stretched it forth, and it was restored whole, like the other. The Pharisees left and held a council against Him about how they might destroy Him (Matthew 12:9–14).

Jesus withdrew from the synagogue with His disciples and went to the sea. He had a great multitude following Him because of His healings, and they had heard what great things He did. They pressed against Him to touch Him, as many had plagues and unclean spirits. When they saw Him, they fell down before Him and cried, saying, "Thou art the Son of God." And He charged them that they should not make Him known (Mark 3:7–12).

Jesus then went up the mountain, and He ordained twelve of the disciples to be apostles: they included Simon, who was surnamed Peter; James, son of Zebedee; John, brother of James, Andrew, and Philip; Bartholomew; Matthew; Thomas; and James, the son of Alphaeus; Simon the Canaanite; and Judas Iscariot, who also betrayed him. Then they went into a house (Luke 6:12–16).

He taught them by saying,

Blessed are the poor in spirit: for theirs is the kingdom of heaven.

Blessed are they that morn: for they shall be comforted.

Blessed are the meek: for they shall inherit the earth.

Blessed are they which do hunger and thirst after righteousness: for they shall be filled.

Blessed are the merciful: for they shall obtain mercy.

Blessed are the pure in heart: for they shall see God.

Blessed are the peacemakers: for they shall be called children of God.

Blessed are they which are persecuted for righteousness' sake: for theirs is the kingdom of heaven.

Blessed are ye, when men shall revile you, and persecute you and shall say all manner of evil against you falsely, for my sake.

Rejoice and be exceedingly glad: for great is your reward in heaven, for so persecuted are the prophets which were before you (Matthew 5:1–12).

TEACHINGS

You are the light of the world so let your light shine before Me, that they may see your good works and glorify your Father, who is in heaven (Matthew 5:16).

Jesus tells them that He has not come to destroy the law or the prophets, "I have not come to destroy, but to fulfill"(Matthew 5:17). Your righteousness shall exceed the righteousness of the scribes and Pharisees, or you shall in no case enter the kingdom of heaven. Jesus did not speak against the law itself but against the abuses and excesses to which it had been subjected. Our righteousness must: 1) come from what God does in us, not what we can do by ourselves; 2) be God-centered, not self-centered; 3) be based on reverence for God, not approval from people; and 4) go beyond keeping the law to living by the principles behind the law.

We should be as concerned about our attitudes. Killing and anger violate God's command to love. Anger always leads to violence, emotional hurt, increased mental stress, and spiritual damage. Self-control is good, but Christ wants us to practice thought-control as well. Jesus said we would be accountable even for our attitudes. If we have a grievance with a friend, we need to resolve the problem as soon as possible. Our attitudes toward others reflect our relationship with God. We must get things right with our brothers and sisters before we stand before God.

Jesus says, "Whoever looks at a woman to lust for her already committed adultery with her in his heart" "(Matthew 5:28). Acting out sinful desire is harmful in spiritual ways: 1) it causes people to excuse sin rather than to stop sinning; 2) it destroys marriages; 3) it is a deliberate rebellion against God's Word; and 4) it always hurts someone else in addition to the sinner. Sinful actions are more dangerous than sinful desires.

Divorce is as hurtful and destructive today as in Jesus' day. God intends marriage to be a lifetime commitment (Genesis 2:24). Jesus said that divorce is not permissible except for unfaithfulness. The word "fornication" implies a sexually immoral lifestyle, not a confessed and repented act of adultery. If you find out your partner has been unfaithful, you are well-advised first to pray and then make every effort to forgive, reconcile, and restore the relationship.

In teaching vows, Jesus emphasized the importance of telling the truth. The Bible condemns making vows or taking oaths casually, giving your word while knowing that you will not keep it, or swearing falsely in God's name. Jesus told His followers not to use vows or oaths—their word alone should be enough (James 5:12). If we tell the truth, we will not have to back it up with "I promise."

Revenge laws were to limit vengeance and help the court administer punishment that was neither too strict nor too lenient. We still say, "I was just doing to him what he did to me." Our desire should not be to keep score or even the score but to love and forgive. This is not natural to us but supernatural instead. Only God can give us the strength to love as He does. Instead of planning vengeance, pray for those who hurt you and pray for the strength and ability to forgive no matter how difficult it will be for you to do so. Jesus feels it is more important to give justice and mercy than to receive it.

Be loving by praying for our enemies; this will overcome evil with good. The Pharisees thought they should love only those who love in return and hate their enemies. But Jesus says we are to love our enemies and treat them well; then you will truly show that Jesus is Lord of your life. This is only possible for those who give themselves fully to God because only He can deliver people from natural hatred and selfishness. We must trust the Holy Spirit to help us show love to those for whom we may not feel love.

Be of good cheer when you give or tithe. Do not be a hypocrite, as used in this text to describe people who do good acts for appearance only, not out of compassion or other good motives. These empty acts are their only reward. But God will reward those who are sincere in their faith. The standard tithe of God is ten percent of the first fruits, not after taking your payroll tax or if a business is using your net income. This is off the top in secret, and you will be rewarded by God.

Prayer is not a public style but private communion with God. There is a place for public prayer, but to pray only where others will notice you indicates that your real audience is not God. Repetition of the same words over and over is no way to ensure that God will hear your prayer. Jesus encourages persistent prayer, but you need to remember all your blessings were taken care of at the cross. You should have a positive attitude when you come to Jesus with your requests, that they are of a sincere heart, and you are asking Him to fulfill your request from the blessings that are already done, and you are asking to receive it in Jesus' name. Be sure you mean what you say. Prayers should be with praise first, worship, and then praise.

"Thy will be done" allows us to offer ourselves as doers of God's will, asking Him to guide, lead, and give us the means to accomplish His purpose. We must trust God daily to provide what He knows we need. Ask God to help you recognize temptation and to strengthen you to overcome it and choose God's way. Jesus tells us if we do not forgive others, God will also refuse to forgive us. We are all sinners in God's eyes. After you have said your prayers, please end with, "In Jesus' name. Amen."

Your fasting should not be in front of men, but to your Father who is in the secret place; your Father who sees in secret will reward you openly. Jesus fasted forty days and forty nights in the wilderness; afterward, He was hungry. When you eat and drink, do not eat and drink for yourselves. You fast for strife and debate and to strike with the fist of wickedness—a day for a man to afflict his soul.

Money, or another word, mammon, is something you should not serve. Money or treasures you think are so important can be corrupt, stolen, and evil. We are meant to serve one master, and that is God. Do you serve money more than God? You should lay up for yourselves treasures in heaven, where nothing can happen to them. No man can serve two masters, for either he will hate the one and love the other, or else he will hold to the one and despise the other. We cannot serve God and mammon!

Worry gives way to ill effects. Jesus tells us not to worry about those needs that God promises to supply. God supplies all the needs of the sparrows, so are you not more important to God than the sparrows? Worry may: 1) damage your health, 2) disrupt your productivity, 3) negatively affect the way you treat others, and 4) reduce your ability to trust in God. The difference between worry and genuine concern is that it immobilizes, and concern moves you to action. Planning for tomorrow is time well spent; worrying about tomorrow is time wasted. Planning is careful thinking about goals, steps, and schedules and then trusting in God's guidance, which can come from us trusting the Holy Spirit. Worries are consumed by fear and make it difficult to trust God.

Judging is for us to examine our motives and conduct instead of judging others. Judge yourself first, and then lovingly forgive and help your neighbor. We need to trust God to be the final judge. We should not stop giving God's Word to unbelievers, but we should be wise and discerning in our witness so that we will not be wasting our time and will not be banging on doors that are bolted.

Ask, seek, and you will find; knock, and it shall be opened to you: for everyone that asks receives; and he that seeks finds; and to him that knocks, it shall be opened. All blessings have already been stored in heaven, and while you ask, also state you receive the blessing in Jesus' name. Amen.

The Golden Rule is all things whatsoever you would want men to do for you, do you even so to them; for this is the law and the prophets.

Way to Heaven (Matthew 7:13–14)

"Enter by the narrow gate; for wide is the gate and broad is the way that leads to destruction, and there are many who go in by it. Because narrow is the gate and difficult is the way which leads to life, and there are few who find it" (Matthew 7:13–14).

Fruit in a person's life is like a good tree that cannot bring forth evil fruit; neither can a corrupt tree bring forth good fruit. Only those who do the will of the Father, who is in heaven, shall enter the kingdom of heaven. Corrupt trees are teachers who deliberately teach false doctrine. An example is them telling you to do good to get good. Wrong! Jesus died at the cross for us, forgiving our sins and presenting our experience for salvation with Him through our belief and our experiences like His, asking forgiveness of our sins. What you do cannot be separated from what you believe. Faith in Christ is what will count at the judgment. "That day" is the final day of reckoning when God will settle all accounts, judging sin and rewarding faith.

After a day of healing, a Centurion's servant came to a city called Nain. His disciples and many people were with him. When he came to the gate of the city, there was a dead man being carried out, the only son of his mother, and she was a widow. When Jesus saw her, He had compassion on her and said unto her, "Weep not." Then He came and touched the coffin stand, and they that carried him stood still. And He said, "Young man, I say unto thee, arise." And he who was dead sat up and began to speak. And He delivered him to his mother. And there came a fear on all; and they glorified God, saying,

"A great prophet is risen up among us"; and, "God had visited His people" (Luke 7:11–16).

One of the Pharisees desired Jesus would eat with him. Jesus went into the Pharisee's house and sat down to eat. Behold, a woman in the city, who was a sinner, knew Jesus sat with the Pharisees, but she brought an alabaster box of ointment, stood behind Him weeping, and she began to wash His feet with tears; then she did wipe them with the hairs of her head; kissed His feet; anointed them with the ointment which was very costly. The Pharisee told Him the woman was a sinner. Jesus gave a story about a creditor who had two debtors: the one owed five hundred pence; the other fifty. When they had nothing to pay, he frankly forgave them both. "Tell Me, therefore, which of them will love him most?" Simon answered, "I suppose the one whom he forgave the most." Jesus said to him that he rightly judged. He said, "I entered into this house, and you gave me no water for My feet, but she has washed My feet with tears; she wiped them with the hairs of her head; she anointed My head with oil." Jesus said to her that her many sins were forgiven because she loved much. Jesus said to her, "Your sins are forgiven. Your faith has saved you. Go in peace" (Luke 7:36–50).

Religious leaders accused Jesus of getting His power from Satan. Jesus knew their thoughts and said unto them, "Every kingdom that is divided against itself is brought to desolation, and every city or house that is divided against itself will not stand. If Satan casts out Satan, he is divided against himself. How shall then his kingdom stand? And if I by Beelzebub cast out devils, by whom do your children cast them out? Therefore, they shall be your judges. But if I cast out devils by the Spirit of God, then the kingdom of God has come to you" (Matthew 12:25–28). "I say to you all manner of sin and blasphemy shall be forgiven to men, but the blasphemy against the Holy Spirit shall not be forgiven unto men. Whosoever speaks a word against the Son of Man, it shall be forgiven him; but whosoever speaks against the Holy Ghost, it will not be forgiven him, either in this world or in the world to come" (Matthew 12:31–32).

PARABLES

All these things Jesus spoke to the multitude in parables: and without a parable He did not speak to them, that it might be fulfilled which was spoken by the prophet saying:

"I will open My mouth in parables: I will utter things kept secret from the foundation of the world."

Matthew 13:34–35

Parable: *The Sower*

"A sower went out to sow his seed. And as he sowed, some fell by the wayside; and it was trampled down, and the birds of the air devoured it. Some fell on rock; and as soon as it sprang up, it withered away because it lacked moisture. And some fell among thorns and the thorns sprang up with it and choked it. But others fell on good ground, sprang up, and yielded a crop a hundredfold." When He had said these things He cried, "He who has ears to hear, let him hear!"

Then the disciples asked Him, saying, "What does this parable mean?" And He said, "To you, it has been given to know the mysteries of the kingdom of God, but to the rest it is given in parables that,

'Seeing they may not see; and hearing they may not understand.'"

"Now the parable is this: The seed is the Word of God. Those by the wayside are the ones who hear; then the devil comes and takes away the Word out of their hearts, lest they should believe and be saved. But the ones on the rock are those who, when they hear, receive the Word with joy; and these have no root, who believe for a while and in time of temptation fall away. Now the ones that fell among thorns are those who, when they have heard, go out and are choked with cares, riches, and pleasures of life and bring no fruit to maturity. But the ones that fell on the good ground are those who, having heard the Word with a noble and good heart, keep it and bear fruit with patience."

Luke 8:4–15

Parable: *The Tares (weeds)*

Jesus said to them: "The kingdom of heaven is like a man who sowed good seed in his field; but while men slept, his enemy came and sowed tares among the wheat and went his way. But when the grain had sprouted and produced a crop, then the tares also appeared. So the servants of the owner came and said to Him, "Sir, did you not sow good seed in your field? How then does it have tares?" He said to them, "An enemy has done this." The servants said to him, "Do you want us then to go and gather them up?" But he said, "No, lest while you gather up the tares you also uproot the wheat with them. Let both grow together until the harvest, and at the time of harvest, I will say to the reapers, 'First gather together the tares and bind them in bundles to burn them, but gather the wheat into my barn.'"

Matthew 13:24–35

Parable: *The Mustard Seed*

Another parable He put forth to them, saying: "The kingdom of heaven is like a mustard seed, which a man took and sowed in his field, which is the least of all the seeds; but when it is grown it is greater than the herbs and becomes a tree, so that the birds of the air come and nest in the branches."

Matthew 13:31–32

The Parable of the Tares Explained

The disciples asked Him to explain the parable of the tares of the field.

He answered and said to them: "He who sows the good seed is the Son of Man. The field is the world, the good seeds are the sons of the kingdom, but the tares are the sons of the wicked one. The enemy who sowed them is the devil, the harvest is the end of the age, and the reapers are the angels. Therefore, as the tares are gathered and burned in the fire, so it will be at the end of this age. The Son of Man will send out His angels, and they will gather out of His kingdom all things that offend, and those who practice lawlessness, and will cast them into the furnace of fire. There will be wailing and gnashing of teeth. Then the righteous will shine forth as the sun in the kingdom of their Father. He who has ears to hear, let him hear!"

Matthew 13:37–43

Parable: *A Girl Restored to Life and a Woman Healed (Mark 5:21–43)*

When Jesus was passed over again by ship to the other side, one of the rulers of the synagogue fell at His feet, asking Him greatly, saying, "My little daughter is at the point of death." He said, "I pray Thee, come lay hands on her." Jesus left with many people following along, and along the way, a woman who had an issue of blood for twelve years pressed behind Jesus and touched His garment. She thought if she touched His clothes, she would be cured, and she would be healed of the plague. Jesus said, "Who touched My clothes?" and she fell to the floor before Him and told Him all the truth. Jesus told her that her faith had made her whole, to go in peace. While speaking, this ruler of the synagogue was met by those who told him his daughter was dead. When Jesus heard this, He told the ruler, "Be not afraid, only believe." When He got to the house, there was weeping and wailing. Jesus asked them, "Why make you this ado and weep? The damsel is not dead; she is sleeping." He put them all out, took the father and mother of the damsel and them that were with Jesus, and entered where the damsel was lying. Jesus took her hand and said to her, "*Talitha, cumi,*" which is being interpreted, "Damsel, I say unto thee, arise." And right away, the damsel arose and walked; she was twelve years old.

Parable: *Two Blind Men Healed* and *A Mute Man Speaks* (Matthew 9:27–34)

But the Pharisees said Jesus cast out devils through the prince of devils because there were two blind men who followed Him crying and saying, "Thou, son of David, have mercy on us!" Jesus asked them if they believed He could heal them, and they said, "Yes, Lord." He touched their eyes, and their eyes were opened. Jesus told them not to let man know it, but they spread abroad everything He had done, including a mute man who was possessed by a devil. Jesus cast out the devil, and the mute man spoke, and that made the people following Him marvel.

Parable: *The Twelve Apostles* (Matthew 10:1–23)

Jesus gave His twelve disciples power against unclean spirits to cast them out and to heal all manner of sickness and all manner of disease. Jesus sent them to the house of Israel, telling them on the way to preach, saying, "The kingdom of heaven is at hand. Heal the sick, cleanse the lepers, raise the dead, cast out devils; freely you have received, freely give" (Matthew 10:7–8). Jesus said, "Give no gifts and look for workmen who are worthy of their message in each town and then stay with them." Jesus told them they would be sheep among wolves. He told them to be wise as serpents and harmless as doves. He advised they would be brought up against governors and kings and instructed them to not worry about what or how to speak because the Spirit of the Father would speak through them. They would be hated by all, for Jesus' sake. If they got persecuted, they were to flee to another town. We, as born-again Christians, will be persecuted, too. Turn to Jesus, counting the cost of following Christ.

Who May Oppose Us	Natural Responses	Possible Pressures	Needed Truth
Government (Matthew 10:17)	Fear & worry	Threats (Matthew 10:1)	The truth will be revealed (Matthew 10:26).
Religious people (Matthew 10:17)		Public records	God's personal will acknowledges us if we acknowledge Him (Matthew 10:32).

Family (Matthew 10:21)		Rejection by loved ones (Matthew 10:34–37)	God's love can sustain us (Matthew 10:31).

*Parable: **John the Baptist Beheaded** (Matthew 14:1–12)*

Herod's illegal marriage to his brother's wife, Herodias, caused him to dislike his sins being known to others. John the Baptist made his sin known to all the people, so Herod threw him in prison. Herod knew John always spoke the truth, and eventually, after all his preaching about Herodias, his wife agreed that with her consent, her daughter could have John's head cut off and placed on a platter after his execution. When Herod heard about Jesus, he threatened Him on His final journey to Jerusalem. Jesus would not speak to Herod, so Herod responded with mocking and spite.

God can reveal Himself in various ways to get our attention. He can use the Word, our minds, other people, or other events. God is persistent and persuasive, but He is never forceful with us. If we miss His message, it is a tragedy. Do you wait for God to respond, and do you welcome Him?

*Parable: **Feeding the Five Thousand** (Matthew 14:13–23)*

Jesus, hearing all these things, departed with the disciples to a deserted place by ship. When Jesus came out and saw all the people, He felt compassion that His preaching had lasted all day, and they were hungry. The disciples wanted Him to send them to the village, but He asked them how many loaves they had. When the disciples knew, they told Jesus, "Five loaves and two fish." Jesus told them to have the multitude sit down on the grass. Jesus then looked up to heaven and blessed and broke the loaves and the two fish, and all ate and were filled. Then they took up twelve baskets from feeding the five thousand men. Jesus told His disciples to get in a ship and go to the other side while Jesus went to disperse the multitudes. He went up to the mountain to pray until evening.

Parable: *Jesus Walks on the Sea (Matthew 14:22–33)*

In the meantime, the disciples in the ship were tossed around by the sea. Jesus later walked across the sea to get to them. The disciples thought it was a spirit and cried out in fear. Jesus said to them, "Be of good cheer; it is I; be not afraid." God does not want us to worry or be afraid. Depend on Him.

Peter answered Jesus with a bid for Him to walk on water, and Jesus told him to come. Peter, with his full faith, walked on water, but when he saw a big wind, he lost faith and became afraid. When he was sinking, he cried out to be saved, so Jesus immediately gave him His hand, but Jesus told him he had no faith. Then when they got in the boat, the wind ceased.

We are to trust Jesus unconditionally for everything. Are we not more important than the sparrows in the sky? Jesus supplies everything for them, and He will supply all our needs if we have no doubt. We must put Jesus first over everything and everyone. God has given us free will to make decisions, but we must be patient to listen for the right direction to proceed. No amount of possessions, money, or gifts is as important as Jesus. God says, "You came by dust, and you will return to dust," so always keep Jesus first.

Parable: *The Bread from Heaven* (John 6:22–40)

The people, realizing Jesus and His disciples had left, took a ship to Capernaum seeking Jesus. They asked Jesus when He had arrived. Jesus announced to them that they were only seeking Him for the loaves He gave them, not for the faith He was giving them for everlasting life as He shall give to us. The people asked what work they might do for the works of God. He told them it wasn't their works but that they believed in Him, whom God had sent.

Jesus told them He is the true bread from heaven. For the bread of God was Jesus, who came down from heaven and gave life unto the world. The people asked for the bread. Jesus told them He was the bread of life, and if they went to Him, they would never hunger or thirst. Jesus told them He came down from heaven not to do His will but the will of God. He said, "If you believeth on Me, you may have everlasting life and be raised up at the last day." Jesus told them His bread came down from heaven that they may eat and not die like their fathers in the wilderness died.

Jesus is the living bread from heaven that if you eat of it (which represents His flesh), drink of his blood (which is represented in our day as grape juice at our Communion), you will have eternal life and be raised up on the last day.

Parable: **Rejected by His Own** *(John 6:41–59)*

His disciples found this hard to hear. Jesus asked if it offended them. He said, "It is the Spirit that quickens, the flesh profits nothing; the words that I speak to you, they are Spirit, and they are life."

Parable: **Many Disciples Turn Away** *(John 6:60–71)*

Some of the disciples could not believe, and one would betray Jesus (John 6:64). From this time, many of the disciples left Him. Then Jesus asked the twelve disciples if they were staying. Then Simon Peter asked Him, "What would we do when You have the words of eternal life? We do believe You are the Christ." Jesus answered them that He chose the twelve even if one among them was a devil. It was Judas Iscariot who betrayed Him.

Parable: **Defilement Comes from Within** *(Matthew 15:1–20)*

The Pharisees and the scribes asked Jesus why His disciples did not wash their hands before eating. Jesus replied to them, "Why do you break the commandment to honor your father and mother?" Because of defiling this commandment, they were to be put to death. He called the multitude, letting them know that if a deed is not planted by the Father, it shall be uprooted. Leave the Pharisees alone. Anytime blind leaders lead the blind, both will fall into a ditch. Afterward, Jesus told them whatever enters the mouth goes into the stomach and is eliminated, but the things which come out of the mouth come from the heart, and they defile a man. For out of the heart proceed evil thoughts, murders, adulteries, fornications, thefts, false witnesses, blasphemies. But Jesus told them that not washing hands did not defile the disciples (Matthew 15:19).

Parable: *A Gentile Shows Her Faith (Matthew 15:21–28)*

When Jesus left and went to the region of Tyre, a woman from Canaan cried out to Him that she had a daughter who was severely demon-possessed. The disciples wanted to send her away, but Jesus told them He was not sent to just the lost sheep of Israel. She pleaded, "Lord, help me!" Jesus told her it was not good to take the children's bread and throw it at the little dogs. She replied, "Yes, Lord, yet even the little dogs eat the crumbs which fall from the owner's table." Jesus answered and said to her, "O woman, great is your faith! Let it be to you as you desire." The multitude had been with Him for three days without eating. The disciples had seven loaves and a few little fish, but Jesus fed four thousand and took up seven large baskets of pieces that were left. Then they got in the boat and sailed to Magdala.

Parable: *Beware of the Leaven of the Pharisees and Herod (Mark 8:13–21)*

When the disciples forgot to take bread, Jesus warned them of the leaven of the Pharisees and of the leaven of Herod. The disciples thought it was their fault because they had forgotten, but Jesus was trying to get them to have faith to trust Him for their loaves and fish. Like when He fed the five thousand before and the four thousand. He could not understand why they did not know.

Parable: **A Blind Man Healed at Bethsaida** *(Mark 8:22–26)*

He went to Bethsaida and led a blind man out of town by the hand, and when he spat on his eyes, the man could see men as trees, walking. He spat on them again, and his eyes were restored. Jesus told him to go home and not to tell anyone in town.

Parable: **Peter Confesses Jesus as the Christ** *(Mark 8:27–30)*

They left Bethsaida for the coasts of Caesarea Philippi. Jesus asked the disciples who men said that He was. They answered, "John the Baptist, one of the prophets, or some said, Elijah." Then Jesus asked the disciples who they thought He was. Peter told Him He was the Christ, the Son of the living God. Jesus blessed Peter and told him it could only have been revealed by His Father, who was in heaven. Jesus told him He upon that rock would build His church and the gates of hell would not prevail against it; that whatever they bound on earth would be bound in heaven, and whatever they loosed on earth would be loosed in heaven, but they should tell no man that He was Jesus the Christ.

Parable: **Jesus Transfigured on the Mount** *(Matthew 17:1–13)*

Now, after six days, Jesus took His brothers Peter, James, and John and led them high upon a mountain where they could be by themselves. Then Jesus was transformed before them. His face shone like the sun, and His clothes became as white as light. Moses and Elijah appeared before them, talking to Jesus. Peter answered that it was good for them to be there and that they should build three tabernacles: one for Jesus, one for Moses, and one for Elijah. While Peter was speaking, a bright cloud overshadowed them; and suddenly, out of the cloud, God spoke, saying, "This is My Son in whom I am well pleased. Hear Him!" (Matthew 3:17). The disciples fell on their faces and were frightened. Jesus went to them, touched them, and said, "Arise, and do not be afraid" (Matthew 17:7). When they opened up their eyes, they only saw Jesus. On their way down the mountain, Jesus told them not to tell anyone about the vision until the Son of Man had risen from the dead. His disciples wanted to know why Elijah was to come first. Jesus told them Elijah would restore all things. The scribes did what they wanted to Elijah, just like they were going to do to Jesus. He would suffer at their hands like John the Baptist.

Parable: *A Boy Is Healed* (Matthew 17:14–21)

After coming down the mountain, they met the multitude, and with them was a man asking Jesus to have mercy on his son because he was an epileptic. He often would fall into the fire and often into the water. The man told Jesus he had taken him to the disciples, but they could not cure him. Jesus called the disciples faithless and a perverse generation. Jesus asked them how long He had to be with them for their belief that they could heal. Jesus rebuked the demon, and it came out of him, and the child was cured. The disciples asked why they could not cure him, and Jesus said to them, "Because of your unbelief." If they or if you have faith, you can do all impossible things.

Parable: **Jesus Again Predicts His Death and Resurrection** *(Matthew 17:22–23)*

Now while they were staying in Galilee, Jesus told the disciples He was about to be betrayed into the hands of men, and they would kill Him, but on the third day, He would be raised up. The disciples were very sad at that thought. When they went to Capernaum, the temple tax collector went to Peter and said, "Does your Teacher not pay the temple tax?" (Matthew 17:24). Peter said yes and went to Jesus. Jesus asked him if the kings of the earth take customs or taxes from their sons or from strangers. Peter answered, "From strangers," and Jesus told him the sons were free. Not offending them, Jesus sent Peter to cast a hook, take the fish that came first, open the mouth, get the piece of money and take it to the temple tax collector for him and Jesus.

Parable: **Of the Lost Sheep**

Jesus tells us that when a shepherd has a hundred sheep, and one comes up missing, he will surely look for the one lost sheep. Jesus rejoiced more over the one lost sheep than the ninety-nine who were safe. "Even so, it is not the will of your Father, who is in heaven, that one of these little ones should perish" (Matthew 18:14).

Now, if your brother trespasses against you, go tell him his fault alone. Just you and him. If he does not hear you, take two or three witnesses so the trespass can be substantiated. If he does not hear you, then take it to the church. If he neglects to hear the church, let him be as a heathen man. "For where two or three are gathered in My name, there am I with them" (Matthew 18:20).

Peter asked Jesus how many times his brother should sin against him and still forgive him; seven times? "No," Jesus said, "until seventy times seven."

Parable: *Unforgiving Debtor*

A certain king took account of his servants for debt. One owed him ten thousand talents, but he could not pay. His lord commanded him to be sold, and his wife, and children, and all he had, and payment to be made. The debtor fell down and worshipped his lord, asking for patience, and he told him that he would pay all of the debt. The lord took compassion on him and forgave him of his debt. The same servant went out and found one of his fellow servants who owed him a hundred pence, and he laid his hands on him and took him by the throat, saying, "Pay me what you owe." His fellow servant fell down at his feet, asked for patience with him, and said he would pay it all. But instead of forgiving him, the fellow servant was cast in prison. When his fellow servants saw what he had done to the fellow servant, they told the lord all that was done. The lord delivered him to the tormentors until he paid the debt, all that was due. Your Heavenly Father will also do this to you if you, from your hearts, forgive not every one of your brothers' trespasses.

Jesus walked in Galilee, not Judea, because the Jews wanted to kill Him. It was the time for the Jewish celebration of the Feast of Tabernacles. His brethren told Him to go to Judea so that His disciples would see the works He had done. There is not a man that does anything in secret while he seeks to be known openly. They said, "Show Yourself to the world" because His brethren did not believe in Him. Then Jesus said unto them, "My time is not yet come: but your time is always ready. The world will not hate you, but they do Me because I testify that the works thereof are evil" (John 7:6–7). Jesus did not go to the feast because it was not His time. Jesus had not filled His purpose.

After the brethren went to the feast, Jesus, in secret, taught in the temple. The Jews wanted to know how He learned letters, having never learned. Jesus told them His doctrine was not His, but from Him that sent Him. "If any man wills to do His will, he shall know of the doctrine, whether it be God or whether I speak of Myself. A man who speaks of himself seeks his own glory, but he who seeks the glory of the One who sent him is true, and no unrighteousness is in him" (John 7:17–18). Jesus asked them why they sought to kill Him instead of being righteous to Moses' law. Those who went about to kill Him said He had a devil. You are to judge not according to appearance but only judge righteously.

Then some from Jerusalem asked if this was He who they sought to kill. Then discussion came because He knew when He was coming, but the Jews did not know when Christ would come. Jesus told them that they knew Him, and they knew when He'd come: "I do not come from Myself, but He that sent Me is true, whom you know not" (John 7:28). Jesus told them He knew who He was and that He had sent Him. Then they sought to take Him, but no man laid hands on Him because His hour was not yet here. The people believed in Him but said that when Christ came, He would do more miracles than Jesus.

Jesus went to the Mount of Olives, and early in the morning, He went again to the temple to sit down and teach the people. Then the scribes and Pharisees brought Him a woman caught in adultery. They told Jesus she was caught in the act of adultery. The law of Moses stated she should be stoned, and this would give them something to accuse Jesus. They asked Jesus, "What do You say?" Jesus stooped down and, with His finger, wrote on the ground as if He had not heard them. When they kept asking, Jesus stood up and said that any of them that is without sin, let him cast a stone at her; then Jesus bent down again to write on the ground. And those who heard this, being convicted by their own conscience, left. Jesus was left alone with the woman, and when Jesus lifted up and saw no one but the woman, He said to her, "Where are your accusers? Did not one condemn you?" And she told Jesus, "No man, Lord." Jesus told her, "Neither do I condemn you, so go and sin no more."

Jesus told the Pharisees that He was the light of the world and whoever followed Him would not walk in darkness. The Pharisees told Jesus He bore a record of Himself and His record was not true, but Jesus told them His record was true because He knew where He came from and where He'd go. Jesus told the Pharisees that they judge after the flesh, but Jesus judges no man. "If I did judge, My judgment is true because I am not alone, but I am with the Father who sent Me" (John 8:16). Jesus told them they did not know Him or His Father.

No one laid hands on Him because His hour was not yet come. "'I do nothing of Myself; but as My Father taught Me, I speak these things. My Father has not left Me alone, for I always do those things that please Him.' As Jesus spoke these things, many believed in Him" (John 8:28–30).

A certain lawyer tempted Jesus to know what he should do to inherit eternal life. Jesus asked him what was written in the law and how he read it. The lawyer said, "You should love your God with all your heart, all your soul, with all your strength, all your mind, and love your neighbor as yourself." Jesus said to him that he had answered right, so if he did this, he would live. The lawyer asked who his neighbor was. Jesus answered in a parable.

Parable: *The Good Samaritan*

There was a man who was walking from Jerusalem to Jerico, and some thieves stripped him of everything he had, wounded him, and departed, leaving him half dead. Then a priest came down the road and, seeing the wounded man, crossed to the other side. Likewise, a Levite did the same thing as the priest. A Samaritan came where he was and had compassion for him; he fixed his wounds, pouring in oil and wine, and set him on his own beast. He took him to an inn, took care of him, and told the innkeeper to give him all that he needed, and he would pay any overage when he came back through. Jesus asked which of these three was the good neighbor. The answer, of course, was the Samaritan, so Jesus said, "Then go, and do the same."

Jesus went on His way and entered a village where a certain woman named Martha received Him into her house. She had a sister, Mary, who also sat at His feet to hear His Word. Martha was concerned about serving Jesus, so she went to Jesus to ask if He did not care that her sister had left her to serve alone. And Jesus answered and said to her, "Martha, Martha, you are careful and troubled about many things, but one thing is needful, and Mary has chosen that good part, which shall not be taken away from her" (Luke 10:41–42).

The disciples asked Jesus to teach them to pray, as John also taught his disciples. And He said to them,

> When you pray, say, "Our Father in heaven, Hallowed be Your name, Your kingdom come, Your will be will be done on earth as it is in heaven. Give us this day our daily bread. And forgive us our debts, as we forgive our debtors. And do not lead us into temptation, but deliver us from the evil one. For Yours is the kingdom and the power and the glory forever. Amen."
>
> Matthew 6:9–13

Jesus warns us about worrying, "Take no thought for your life, what you shall eat; neither for your body, what you shall put on. Your Father knows that you have need of these things. Seek the kingdom of God instead, and they shall be supplied to you" (Matthew 6:31–33). "Fear not, little flock; for it is your Father's good pleasure to give you the kingdom" (Luke 12:32). "For where your treasure is, there will your heart be also" (Luke 12:34).

Jesus told them many times that He would leave this world but would return at some future time. He also said the kingdom was being prepared for His followers. God is delaying His return so more people will have the opportunity to follow Him. Before Jesus comes back, we have time to live out our beliefs and to reflect Jesus' love as we relate to others. Jesus promises a reward for those who have been faithful to the Master. Our heavenly rewards will be the most accurate reflection of what we have done on earth, and they will be far greater than we can imagine. Until the time that Jesus comes back, we must watch for Him, work diligently, and obey His commands. Such attitudes are especially necessary for leaders. Watchful and faithful leaders will be given increased opportunities and responsibilities. Although God will not hold us responsible for gifts He has not given us, all of us have enough gifts and duties to keep us busy until Jesus returns.

Parable: *A Spirit of Infirmity* (Luke 13:10–17)

While Jesus was teaching in the synagogue on the Sabbath, there was a woman who had a spirit of infirmity for eighteen years and was hunched over and could not lift herself up. Jesus called her to Him. He told her she was loosed from her infirmity as He laid hands on her; immediately, she was made straight and glorified God. The ruler of the synagogue was mad because Jesus healed on the Sabbath. Their law said to work six days, including the healing. Jesus called them hypocrites that they said to rest on the Sabbath, but if they lost one of their animals in the stall that they cared for, they would go after the animal. Jesus asked them, "Should not this woman, being a daughter of Abraham, whom Satan bound, be loosed from this bond on the Sabbath?" When He told them these things, all His adversaries were ashamed, and all the people rejoiced for all the glorious things that were done by Him.

Parable: *The Parable of the Lost Coin* (Luke 15:8–10)

A woman having ten pieces of silver, if she loses one piece, will sweep the house and seek diligently until she finds it. When she finds the piece of silver, she'll call her friends and her neighbors to rejoice with her. Jesus also said there is joy in the presence of angels of God over one sinner that repented.

Parable: *The Prodigal Son*

There was a certain man who had two sons. The younger son asked his father to give him the portion of goods that he was to inherit. The father complied, so the son left to a far country where he wasted his inheritance on frivolous living. After spending it all, a famine came upon the land, so he became very needy. He joined a citizen of that country, and the citizen sent him into the fields to feed the swine. He had to eat from the husks that the swine ate, and finally, he came to himself and thought about his father's servants. They had bread to eat, so he decided to go home and admit he sinned against heaven and him and that he was not worthy of being called his son, but to please make him a servant. His father told the servants to bring forth the best robe and put it on him and place a ring on his finger and shoes on his feet. After this, the father asked the servants to bring the fatted calf, to kill it, and to let them eat and be merry. While celebrating that his son was lost but now was found, his elder son came home from the field where he was working and asked what these things meant. The servants told him his brother was back, but the son became angry and would not go in. Instead, his father came to him, and the son told him it was not fair because he had been serving him for years. He told his father he never gave him even a kid (goat) that he could party with his friends. The oldest son reminded the father of his brother's sinful life, but the father told him that he had never left him and that all that he had belonged to the oldest brother. He said they should be merry and glad for his brother was dead and is alive again and was lost and is found.

Parable: *The Unjust Steward*

There was a rich man who had a steward that someone made an accusation about that he was wasting his goods. The rich man told him to give an account of his stewardship, or he could not be a steward. The steward thought about not being able to dig, and he was too proud to beg, so he called every one of his master's debtors to him, and he made a deal with each one that if they paid then, he would reduce the amount that they owed the master. The master commended the unjust steward because he had dealt shrewdly. Jesus feels,

He who is faithful in what is least is faithful also in much; and he who is unjust in what is least in unjust also in much. Therefore, if you have not been faithful in the unrighteous mammon (money), who will commit to your trust in the true riches? No servant can serve two masters; for either he will hate the one and love the other; or else he will be loyal to the one and despise the other. You cannot serve God and mammon.

Luke 16:10–13

Parable: *The Rich Man and Lazarus (Luke 17)*

There was a rich man all dressed in purple and fine linen, and every day was great for him. Then there was a certain beggar named Lazarus, who was full of sores and was laid at his gate. He was hoping the rich man would feed him from the crumbs of his table. The dog came and licked his sores. The beggar died and was carried by the angel to Abraham's bosom. The rich man also died and was buried. He was tormented in Hades; he opened his eyes and saw Abraham far off with Lazarus in his bosom. The rich man cried out, asking Abraham to send Lazarus to dip the tip of his finger in water and cool his tongue, for he was tormented by the flame. Abraham told him that those who wanted to pass from there to him could not, nor could those from there pass to them. The rich man wanted Abraham to testify to his brothers so they would not go to Hades. Abraham said to him, "They have Moses and the prophets; let them hear them." And he said, "No, father Abraham, but if one goes to them from the dead, they will repent." But he said to him, "If they do not hear Moses and the prophets, neither will they be persuaded though one rise from the dead."

Parable: *The Death of Lazarus* (*John 11:1–16*)

Lazarus of Bethany, the home of Mary and her sister Martha, was sick. The sisters sent for Him, saying, "Lord, Your beloved friend Lazarus is sick. Could You come right away?" Jesus stayed two days before He left. Finally, Jesus said to the disciples, "We must go to Judea again." The disciples warned Jesus that the Jews wanted to stone Him. Jesus told them it is better to live in the light than stumble in darkness. Jesus told the disciples that their friend Lazarus was asleep, but He needed to go to wake him up from the dead. Thomas said to the disciples, "Let us also go, that we may die with him" (John 11:16).

Then when Jesus went, He found that Lazarus had been laid down in the grave for four days already. Many of the Jews came to console Mary and Martha. When Martha heard Jesus was coming, she went and met Him. Mary sat still in the house. Martha told Jesus if He had been there, her brother would not have died. Martha said she knew that whatsoever you ask of God, God will give it to you. Jesus told her that her brother would rise again, but Martha thought he should rise in the resurrection on the last day. Jesus said to her, "I am the resurrection, and the life. He that believeth in Me, though he were dead, yet shall live: and whosoever liveth and believeth in Me shall never die. Believest thou this?" (John 11:25). The Jews were in the house with Mary, but she rose and left to go where Jesus was, fell down at His feet, and told Him if He had been there, her brother would not have died. When Jesus saw her weeping, and the Jews with her were also weeping, He groaned in the Spirit and was troubled. And He said, "Where have you laid him?" They said to Jesus, "Come and see." Jesus wept. Then the Jews said how He loved Lazarus. Then Jesus, groaning in Himself, told them to take the stone away from the cave. Martha told Jesus he would stink because he had been dead for four days. After the stone was gone, Jesus lifted up His eyes and thanked the Father that He had heard Him, "I knew You heard Me, but because of the people who stood by, I said it, that they may believe that You have sent Me." And when He had spoken, He cried with a loud voice, "Lazarus, come forth." Lazarus came forth in grave clothes, and his face was bound about with a napkin. Jesus told them, "Loose him, and let him go."

Then, some of the Jews who were with Mary and Martha, who were confused and refused to believe, told the Pharisees. They plotted His murder. Because their hearts were so hardened, they chose to reject God instead of admitting they were wrong. They preferred closure instead of being open to God's marvelous power. This shows you that you should beware of your prideful attitudes. They did not want the Romans to lash out at them, but if they were quiet and obedient, they would have partial freedom. The miracles that Jesus did caused a disturbance. One of the Jews, Caiaphas, a high priest, was used by God to explain Jesus' death even though Caiaphas did not realize what he was doing. The Jews' Passover was at hand, and the Jews wondered why Jesus was not coming. The chief priests and the Pharisees had given a command that if anyone knew where Jesus was, they needed to tell them so they could take Him.

God's grace is for everyone. The Pharisees wanted to know when God's kingdom would come, not knowing it had arrived. God's kingdom does not have earthly boundaries. It begins with the work of God's Spirit in people's lives and relationships. We need to look for what God is doing in people's hearts. Many will claim to be the Messiah, so you need to be aware of this. When Jesus returns, your day will be like every other day. No one will need to spread the message because all will see for themselves. We do not know the time of Christ's return, but we know He is coming. Our obedience is to be morally and spiritually ready. Live as if Jesus were returning today. Jesus will come suddenly. Some will be taken to be with Him, and some will be left behind. Keep your commitment to Christ at all times in full strength. Then you will be ready when He returns.

Parable: *The Pharisee and the Tax Collector*

Two men, a Pharisee and a tax collector, went up to the temple to pray. The Pharisee prayed thus with himself, "God, I thank You that I am not like other men—extortioners, unjust, adulterers, or even as this tax collector." The Pharisee said he fasted twice a week. "I give tithes of all that I possess." The tax collector, standing far off, did not raise his eyes to heaven but beat his chest, saying, "God, be merciful to me, a sinner." Jesus said the tax collector went down to his house justified rather than prayed alone like the other. For everyone who exalts himself will be humbled, and he who humbles himself will be exalted.

There was a certain ruler who asked Jesus what he should do to inherit eternal life. Jesus told him, "You know the commandments: 'Do not commit adultery,' 'Do not murder,' 'Do not steal,' 'Do not bear false witness,' 'Honor your father and mother'" (Luke 18:20). The rich man said he had kept all these from his youth. "You still lack one thing. Sell all that you have and distribute to the poor, and you will have treasure in heaven; and come, follow Me" (Luke 18:22). When the rich man heard this, he was very sad. Jesus said, "How hard it is for those who have riches to enter the kingdom of God! For it is easier for a camel to go through the eye of a needle than for a rich man to enter the kingdom of God" (Luke 18:24–25).

Jesus, speaking of marriage and divorce, said God made them male and female. Man would leave his father and mother and cleave to his wife, and they would become one flesh. "What therefore God hath joined together, let not man put asunder" (Mark 10:9). His disciples again asked Him about the same matter. Jesus told them, "Whosoever shall put away his wife and marry another, committeth adultery against her. And if a woman shall put away her husband and be married to another, she committeth adultery" (Mark 10:11–12).

Then little children came to Him, and they thought that He should put His hands on them and pray, but the disciples rebuked those who brought them. Jesus was very displeased with the disciples. "Verily I say unto you, whosoever shall not receive the kingdom of God as a little child, he shall not enter therein. And He took them up in His arms, put His hands upon them, and blessed them" (Mark 10:15–16).

As Jesus entered and passed through Jerico, behold, there was a man named Zacchaeus. He was the chief among the publicans, and he was rich. He wanted to see who Jesus was, but he was too short, so he ran ahead and climbed up into a sycamore tree to see Him because He was coming that way. When Jesus came to the place, He looked up, saw him, and told him to make haste and come down because He was going to stay at his house. When they saw it, they all said that Jesus was gone to be a guest with a man who was a sinner. Zacchaeus told Him he gave half of his goods to the poor, and if he had taken from any man by false accusation, he would restore him fourfold. On this day, salvation came to this house because Zacchaeus was also a son of Abraham. For the Son of man had come to seek and to save that which was lost (Luke 19:10).

Parable: *The Minas (Pound)*

The Jews thought the kingdom of God would appear immediately. When Jesus heard this, He spoke of another parable about the nobleman who went to receive for himself a kingdom and to return. Upon leaving, the nobleman called ten of his servants and said to them, "Do business till I come." His citizens hated him and sent a delegation after him saying, "We will not have this man to reign over us." He had given these servants money so he would learn how much every man had gained by trading. The first servant told him his mina (currency) had earned ten minas. The nobleman told him because he had been a good servant and faithful, he would have authority over ten cities. The second servant told him that his mina had earned five minas, so the nobleman said he would have authority over five cities. Then another came and told him he had kept his mina in a handkerchief. This servant feared the nobleman, and that made the nobleman mad, and he judged him as a wicked servant because he had not even put his money in the bank to draw interest. As the citizens stood by, the nobleman told them to take the mina from him and give it to the one who had ten minas. They said he already had ten. But the nobleman said, "For everyone who had will be given, and from him who does not have, even what he has will be taken away from him." The nobleman said, "But bring those enemies of mine who did not want me to reign over them and slay them before me."

Jesus went on to Jerusalem, and when He drew near to the mountain called Olivet, He sent two of His disciples into the village to find a colt tied. He told them to loosen Him and to bring it back. Jesus told them if anyone asked what they were doing to tell them that the Lord had need of Him. The disciples took the colt to Jesus, put their clothes on Him, and placed Jesus on top. As Jesus was going along, people spread their clothes on the road. When He was near the Mount of Olives, the whole multitude of the disciples began to rejoice, praising God with a loud voice. They praised Him for the mighty works they had seen. The multitudes were saying,

"Blessed is the King who comes in the name of the Lord! Peace in heaven and glory in the highest!" Now, as Jesus came near the city, He wept over it.

Six days before the Passover came to where Lazarus was raised from the dead, and there, they made Him supper, and Martha served it; Lazarus was one who sat with Him at the table. Mary took a pound of ointment, which was very costly, and anointed the feet of Jesus, then wiped His feet with her hair. Judas Iscariot, one of Jesus' disciples, asked Jesus why this ointment was not sold for three hundred pence and given to the poor. He was a thief and did not care about the poor. Jesus told him to leave Mary alone. He said she had kept the ointment for His burying. He said, "The poor you have with you always, but Me you do not have always" (John 12:8). Many of the Jews came not for Jesus' sake only but that they might see Lazarus, who was raised from the dead. The chief priests consulted that they might put Lazarus to death because Jesus had raised Lazarus from the dead, and many of the Jews left the resurrection, went away, and believed in Jesus.

Then the Pharisees decided to meet and see how they could get Jesus engaged in His talk. The Pharisees sent their disciples with the Herodians, saying, "Master, we know that You are true, and teach the way of God in truth, though not caring for any man: because You do not regard the person of man. Jesus, tell us if it is lawful to give tribute to Caesar or not." Jesus, knowing their wickedness, asked them why they were tempting Him and called them hypocrites. He told them to show Him the money. They brought Him a penny, and Jesus asked them whose picture was on the penny. They told Him, "Caesar's." Jesus then told them to give Caesar's money to him and to give God's to God. After the Pharisees heard this, they marveled and went on their way.

The Sadducees came to Jesus about the resurrection. They told Jesus a man died with no children; his brother should marry the widow and raise up seeds for his brother. There were six brothers who all died, so the woman was left, but then she died, too. They asked Jesus in the resurrection whose wife of the seven would she be because they all had her. Jesus told them they knew not resurrection, but if they did, they would know God is not the God of the dead but of the living. After hearing this, the multitude was astonished.

After the Pharisees heard that Jesus had silenced the Sadducees, they gathered, and a lawyer asked Him a question, "Which is the great commandment in the law?" Jesus answered, "The first and great commandment is, Thou shall love the Lord thy God with all thy heart, with all thy soul, and with all thy mind. The second is, Thou shalt love thy neighbor as thyself. On these two commandments hang all the law and the prophets" (Matthew 22:37–40).

Jesus warned the multitude and His disciples that the scribes with their long clothing loved public salutations, and the chief sat in the synagogue and in the rooms where the feasts were being held, which devoured widows' houses, and long prayers, these would receive greater damnation. Jesus sat over against the treasury and noticed how the people cast money into the treasury, and many who were rich cast much. There came a poor widow, and she threw in two mites. Jesus told His disciples about the widow and how she cast in more than the rich. She gave all that she had, even all her living, but the rich only gave a small percentage compared to her.

About fifteen years before the birth of Jesus, Herod the Great remodeled and rebuilt the temple into one of the most beautiful buildings in Jerusalem. He built it not to honor God but to appease the Jews that he ruled. The temple was not finished until 64 AD, but Jesus' prophesy was that no stone would be left standing, and the temple fell in 70 AD when it was completely destroyed by the Romans, also including the city.

The disciples wanted to know when the temple would be destroyed. Jesus gave them a prophetic picture of that time, including events leading up to it. He talked about future events connected with His return to earth to judge all the people. Jesus warned His people about the future so they could learn how to live in the present.

Be spiritually alert and prepared at all times for the return of Jesus. Many have predicted when Jesus will come back, but Christ will return on God's timetable, not ours.

False teachers will always be misled, thinking they have revelations from God. When Jesus returns, we will know beyond doubt because it will be evident to all. Christians have been persecuted in our own land and on foreign mission fields. Persecutions are an opportunity for Christians to witness for Christ to those opposed to Him. God's desire is that the Good News be proclaimed to everyone despite persecution. There is no perfect time. Just remember, God will look out for the welfare of our children just as He has looked out for us. The "elect" are God's chosen people who are saved.

In the end times, it will be hard not to be deceived, but if we are prepared, we can remain faithful. God is the only one who knows what day end time will appear. There will be false teaching and loose morals, which will lead to the loss of true love for God and others. Your love of God is focused on yourself. You cannot truly love if you think only of yourself. The nations of the earth will mourn because unbelievers will suddenly realize they have chosen the wrong side. Everything they have scoffed about will be happening, and it will be too late for them. Heaven is not our only goal, so we need to keep on doing our work until death or until we see the unmistakable return of our Savior. "Weeping and gnashing of teeth" is a phrase used to describe despair. God's coming judgment is as certain as Jesus' return to earth.

God will separate His obedient followers from unbelievers. How we act is our evidence in belief. What we do for others tells us how we really think of Jesus. We should feed the hungry, give the homeless a place to stay, and look after the sick; this will separate us from unbelievers. These acts of mercy can be done daily and do not depend on wealth, ability, or intelligence. Jesus encourages our personal attention to these demands, so there is no excuse to neglect those who have deep needs, and we cannot hand over these demands to the church or government.

After two days, it was the Passover and the Feast of Unleavened Bread, but the chief priests and the scribes plotted how they would take Jesus by trickery and put Him to death. Then one of Jesus' disciples, Judas Iscariot, went to the chief priests to betray Him to them. When they heard Judas, the chief priest and scribes were glad, and they promised to give him money. On the first day of

Unleavened Bread, they killed a lamb and asked Jesus where He wanted the disciples to go and prepare His dinner. He sent out two of His disciples and said to them,

> Go into the city, and a man will meet you carrying a pitcher of water; follow him. Wherever he goes in, say to the master of the house: "The Teacher says, 'Where is the guest room in which I may eat the Passover with My disciples?'" Then he will show you a large upper room, furnished and prepared; there make ready for us.
>
> Mark 14:13–15

His disciples went out and came to the city and found things just as Jesus had told them.

In the evening, the twelve disciples and Jesus sat and ate, but Jesus said to them that one who ate with Him would betray Him. The disciples were sorrowful, and each asked Jesus if it was him.

> "The Son of Man indeed goes just as it is written of Him, but woe to the man by whom the Son of Man is betrayed! It would have been good for that man if he had never been born." And as they were eating, Jesus took bread, blessed and broke it, and gave it to them and said, "Take, eat; this is My body." Then He took the cup, and when He had given thanks, He gave it to them, and they all drank from it. And He said to them, "This is My blood of the new covenant, which is shed for many. Assuredly, I say to you,

I will no longer drink of the fruit of the vine until that day when I drink it new in the kingdom of God." After singing a hymn, they went out to the Mount of Olives.

Mark 14:21–26

Jesus told them they would all be offended because of Him that night. "For it is written, 'I will strike the Shepherd, and the sheep will be scattered.' But after I have been raised, I will go before you to Galilee" (Mark 14:27–28). Peter told Jesus he would not stumble like the rest, but Jesus told him that before the rooster crowed twice, he would deny Jesus three times. Then they went to Gethsemane, and Jesus told His disciples to sit there while He prayed. Jesus took Peter, James, and John with Him, and He began to be troubled and deeply distressed. Then He said to them, "My soul is exceedingly sorrowful, even to death. Stay here and watch" (Mark 14:34). He went a little farther, fell on the ground, and prayed that the hour might pass Him if it was possible. And He said, "Abba, Father, all things are possible for You. Take this cup away from Me; nevertheless, not what I will, but what You will" (Mark 14:36).

Then Jesus went back to the disciples and found them sleeping. And He said to Peter, "Could you not watch one hour without sleeping? Watch and pray, lest you enter into temptation. The spirit indeed is willing, but the flesh is weak" (Mark 14:37–38). He told them the same thing as before, but He left to pray again. When He returned again, they were asleep.

Then He came the third time and said to them, "Are you still sleeping and resting? It is enough! The hour has come; behold, the Son of Man is being betrayed into the hands of sinners. Rise, let us be going, See, My betrayer is a hand." Immediately while He was speaking, Judas, one of the twelve, with a great multitude with swords and clubs, came from the chief priests, scribes, and the elders. Now His betrayer had given them a signal, saying, "Whomever I kiss is the One, seize Him and lead Him away safely." Immediately coming up to Jesus, he said to Him, "Rabbi, Rabbi!" and he kissed Him. Then they laid their hands on Him and took Him. One who stood by drew his sword and stuck the servant of the high priest, and cut off his ear.

Mark 14:41–47

They led Jesus away to the high priest, and with Him were assembled all the priests, the elders, and scribes. Peter followed Him into the courtyard of the high priest, where he sat with the servants in front of the fire. The high priest and all the council looked for a testimony against Jesus to put Him to death, finding none. There were many false witnesses, but not one of them agreed about their testimony. Finally, the high priest stood up and asked Jesus, saying, "Do You answer nothing? What is it these men testify against You?" Jesus kept silent. "Again, the high priest asked Him, saying to Him, 'Are You the Christ, the Son of the Blessed?' Jesus said, 'I am. And you will see the Son of Man sitting at the right hand of the Power and coming with the clouds of heaven'" (Mark 14:61–62). The high priest tore his clothes and said, "Why is there any further need for witnesses?" The high priest declared they had heard blasphemy, so they condemned Him to be deserving of death. Some spit on Him and they blindfolded Him, beat Him, and said to Him, "Prophesy!" And the officers struck Him with the palms of their hands.

While Peter was warming himself by the fire, a girl said, "You also were with Jesus of Nazareth." Peter denied it, saying he did not understand what she was saying. As he went out on the porch, a rooster crowed. The servant girl told those standing by, "This is one of them." Peter denied it again, and then later, those who stood by when the girl said that said to Peter again, "Surely you are one of them; for you are a Galilean, and your speech shows it." Peter began to curse and swear, "I do not know this Man of whom you speak!" A second time the rooster crowed. Then Peter reminded himself that Jesus said to him earlier, "Before the rooster crows twice, you will deny Me three times." Then Peter wept when he thought about what he had said.

The Jewish leaders sent Jesus to Pilate, the Roman governor, because the Romans had taken capital punishment away from the Jews. The Jews wanted Jesus condemned to death, so He had to be condemned by a Roman leader. The Jews wanted Him to be at the cross because they thought this would be God's curse. They wanted to convince the people that Jesus was cursed, not blessed. Pilate asked Him if He was King of the Jews, but Jesus' answer to him was,

"Thou sayest it." The chief priests accused Him of many things, but He answered nothing. Many things were asked of Jesus, but nothing answered, so Pilate marveled.

Now at the feast, the governor was accustomed to releasing one prisoner that they requested. There was one prisoner who was chained with other prisoners because he had committed murder in the rebellion. The multitude asked him to do just as he had always done for them. Pilate answered them, saying, "Do you want me to release the King of the Jews?" Pilate asked them what they wanted to do with Jesus. Pilate knew the chief priests only had envy. The chief priests stirred up the multitude that he should rather release Barnabas to them. Pilate asked them what they wanted to do with Jesus. They cried out, "Crucify Him!" Then Pilate asked, "What evil has He done?" And they cried out all the more, "Crucify Him!" Pilate wanted to gratify the crowd, so he released Barnabas to them and delivered Jesus after he had scourged Him to be crucified.

Then the soldiers led Him away into the hall called Praetorium, and they called together the whole garrison. They clothed Him with a twisted crown of thorns and put it on His head. Then they began to salute Him, "Hail, King of the Jews!" The soldiers struck Him on the head with a reed and spit on Him, and bowing a knee, they worshipped Him. After mocking Him, they took the purple robe off, put His own clothes on, and led Him out to crucify Him. The soldiers compelled Simon, the father of Alexander and Rufus, to bear the cross, and they took Him to the place called Place of a Skull. They gave Him a drink of wine mingled with myrrh, but He did not take it. After crucifying Him, they divided His garments, casting lots for them to determine what every man should take. Now in the third hour, they crucified Him. The inscription of His accusation was written above, "The King of the Jews."

Jesus was crucified with two robbers, one on each of His sides. The scripture was fulfilled, which says, "And He was numbered with the transgressors" (Mark 15:28). And when the sixth hour had come, there was a darkness over all the land until the ninth hour. At the ninth hour, Jesus cried with a loud voice saying, "*Eloi, Eloi, lama, sabachthani*," which is being interpreted as "My God, My God, why have You forsaken Me?" Then someone ran, filled a sponge full of sour wine, put it on the reel, and offered it to Him to drink, saying, "Let Him down." When Jesus, therefore, had received the drink, He said, "It is finished," and He bowed His head and gave up the ghost.

Since it was the Preparation, the bodies should not remain upon the cross on the Sabbath day, so the Jews asked Pilate that their legs might be broken and that they might be taken away. The soldiers broke the legs of the first and of the others who were crucified with Jesus. Then when they came to Jesus, they knew He was already dead, so they did not break His legs. One soldier with a spear pierced his side and forthwith came out blood and water. The soldier saw it, bared record, and His record was true; and he knew Jesus said truth, that you might believe. These things were done so the scripture could be fulfilled: "A bone of Him shall not be broken." Another scripture said, "They shall look on Him whom they have pierced."

When evening came, Joseph, who was one of Jesus' disciples, went to Pilate and begged for the body of Jesus. Pilate demanded the body be delivered. When Joseph had taken the body, he wrapped it in a clean linen cloth and laid it in his own new tomb. Then Joseph rolled a great stone to the door of the opening and departed. Both Marys were sitting in front of the opening. The chief priests and the Pharisees went to Pilate and told him they were afraid Jesus would rise again, so they wanted Him secured. Pilate told them to take care of it on their watch. The chief priests and the Pharisees made sure the stone was sealed and sat someone there to watch. On the first day after the Sabbath, Mary Magdalene and Mary, mother of James, brought sweet spices that they might come and anoint Him. And behold, there was a large earthquake, for the angels of the Lord descended from heaven, and came and rolled back the stone from the door, and sat on it. Upon entering, they saw a young man sitting on the right side, clothed in a long white garment, and they were frightened. He told the women not to be frightened that Jesus was crucified, risen, and was not there. He told them to go quickly, tell the disciples that He had risen from the dead, had gone to Galilee before them, and they shall see Him. The women departed quickly with fear and joy, running to bring His disciples word. As they went to tell His disciples, Jesus met them, saying, "All hail."

Jesus came upon two of them walking to a village of Emmaus, which was from Jerusalem, talking to each other when Jesus drew near them and went with them. He asked, "Why are you walking and talking about your sadness?" They answered Jesus with a question about whether He was a stranger in Jerusalem and knew nothing about what happened. Jesus wanted to know, "What things?" They told Jesus all that had happened. He called them fools that they ought to know Christ would have to suffer to enter His glory. It was late, so they invited Him in to eat and to spend time with them. As He sat at dinner with them, He took bread, blessed it, broke it, and gave it to them. And their eyes opened, and they knew Him, and He vanished out of their sight. They returned to Jerusalem and told the disciples.

Then the same day in the evening, when the doors were shut where the disciples had assembled for fear of the Jews, Jesus came and stood in their midst and said to them, "Peace be with you." Jesus rebuked their unbelief and hardness of heart because they did not believe those who had seen Him after He had risen.

> And He said to them, "Go into all the world and preach the gospel to every creature. He who believes and is baptized will be saved, but he who does not believe will be condemned. And these signs will follow those who believe: In My name, they will cast out demons; they will speak with new tongues; they will take up serpents; and if they drink anything deadly, it will by no means hurt them; they will lay hands on the sick, and they will recover."

> Mark 16:15–18

Thomas, one of the disciples, was not there when Jesus came back to the disciples, so he told them unless he saw on Jesus' hands the print of the nails, put his finger into the print of the nails, and thrust his hand into His side, he would not believe. After eight days again, the disciples with Thomas were assembled, and Jesus came among them. Jesus told Thomas to behold His hands, reach his hand, and thrust it into His side: and be not faithless but believing. Thomas answered, "My Lord and My God." Jesus told Thomas, "Blessed are they that have not seen and yet have believed."

Jesus showed Himself when the disciples Simon Peter, Thomas, and Nathanael of Cana in Galilee, the sons of Zebedee, and two other disciples went fishing but caught nothing. When the morning came, Jesus stood on the shore, but the disciples did not know it was Jesus. Jesus asked them if they had any meat, and they answered, "No." He told them to cast the net on the right side of the ship, and they would find them. They caught so many fish they were not able to draw the multitude of fish. As soon as they came to land, they saw a fire of coals, fish lying there, and bread. Jesus told them to come and dine, and then the disciples knew it was Jesus.

Jesus was together with them, and He commanded them that they should not depart from Jerusalem but wait for the promise of the Father, "Which," saith He, "you have heard from Me. You shall be baptized with the Holy Spirit." The disciples asked Jesus if He would restore again the kingdom of Israel, and He replied, "It is not for you to know the times or the seasons which the Father has put in His own power." After He had spoken all these things, He was taken up, and a cloud received Him out of their sight to set on the right hand of God. And while they stared at heaven, two men stood by them, in white apparel, saying, "Why do you stare up into heaven? This same Jesus, who is taken up from you into heaven, shall so come in like manner as you have seen Him go into heaven" (Acts 1:11).

And they went and preached everywhere, the Lord working in them and confirming the Word through the accompanying signs. Amen (Mark 16:20).

MY PRAYER SUGGESTION

This prayer is to God, so we should always start with "Our Father who art in heaven" because there are many gods, but only one for us.

Our Heavenly Father who art in heaven, we thank You for all creation, including each one of us, in Your image for a certain purpose. We promise there will only be One God, and we thank You for giving us Your only begotten Son and the Holy Spirit. Thank You, Jesus, for our salvation, repentance, eternal life, and for our sitting at Your right side in heaven. We will preach to all the nations; we will cast out demons; serve; lay hands on the sick, and they will recover. We will follow the Holy Spirit for God's instructions to guide, comfort, and give us power, strength, knowledge, and wisdom. Thank You for helping us with humbleness, patience, self-centeredness, self-control, willingness, wellness, kindness, friendliness, faithfulness, holiness, and godliness. We ask this in Your name, Jesus. Amen.

Parable	Matthew	Mark	Luke
The Sower	Matthew 13:3–23	Mark 4:1–20	Luke 8:5–15
The Tares	Matthew 13:24–30	-	-
The Mustard Seed	Matthew 13:31–32	Mark 4:30–32	Luke 13:18–19
The Leaven	Matthew 13:33	-	Luke 13:20–21
The Hidden Treasure	Matthew 13:44	-	-
Parable of the Pearl	Matthew 13:45–46	-	-
The Parable of the Dragnet	Matthew 13:47–50	-	-
The Lost Sheep	Matthew 18:12–14	-	Luke 15:3–7

Unmerciful Servant	Matthew 18:23–35	-	-
Laborers in the Vineyard	Matthew 20:1–16	-	-
The Two Sons	Matthew 21:28–31	-	-
The Wicked Husband-man	Matthew 21:33–43	Mark 12:1–11	Luke 20:9–18
Marriage of the King's Son/The Banquet	Matthew 22:1–14	-	Luke 14:15–24
The Ten Virgins	Matthew 25:1–12	-	-
The Talents	Matthew 25:14–30	-	Luke 19:11–27
Seed Growing Secretly	-	Mark 4:26–29	-

The Two Debtors	-	-	Luke 7:41–47
The Good Samaritan	-	-	Luke 10:30–37
The Rich Fool	-	-	Luke 12:16–21
The Faithful Servant	Matthew 24:42	Mark 13:33–37	Luke 12:35–48
Lost Money	-	-	Luke 15:8–10
The Prodigal Son	-	-	Luke 15:11–32
The Unjust Steward	-	-	Luke 16:1–8
The Rich Man and the Beggar Lazarus	-	-	Luke 16:19–31

Other Examples of Figurative Speech

The Wise and the Foolish Builders	Matthew 7:24–27	-	Luke 6:47–49
The Patch and the Wineskins	Matthew 9:16–17	Mark 2:21–22	Luke 5:36–39
The Strong Man Bound	Matthew 12:29	Mark 3:27	Luke 11:21–22
Jesus' True Relatives	Matthew 12:46–50	Mark 3:31–35	Luke 8:19–21
The Wise and the Foolish Builders	Matthew 7:24–27	-	Luke 6:47–49
The Patch and the Wineskins	Matthew 9:16–17	Mark 2:21–22	Luke 5:36–39

APPENDIX

BOOKS OF THE NEW TESTAMENT

ACTS OF THE APOSTLES:

Author: Luke, a Gentile physician

Purpose: To give an accurate account of the birth and growth of the Christian church.

Features: The story of the men and women who took that commission seriously and began to spread the news of a risen Savior to the remote corners of the known world.

ROMANS:

Author: Paul the Apostle to the Romans

Purpose: While the four Gospels present the words and works of Jesus Christ, Romans explore the significance of His sacrificial death.

Features: Book of theology, practical exhortation, the Good News of Jesus Christ is more than facts to be believed; it is also a life to be lived—a life of righteousness justified by God's grace through the redemption that is in Christ Jesus.

1 CORINTHIANS:

Author: Paul

Purpose: Reveals the problems, pressures, and struggles of a church called out of a pagan society. In addition to works of discipline, Paul shares the words of the council in answer to questions raised by the Corinthian believers.

Features: Addresses problems in their church life, styles, factions, lawsuits, immortality, questionable practices, abuse of the Lord's Supper, and spiritual gifts

2 CORINTHIANS:

Author: Paul

Purpose: He wrote this letter to express his thanksgiving for the repentant majority and to appeal to the rebellious minority to accept his authority. He defends his conduct, character, and calling as an apostle of Jesus Christ.

Features: Swaying by false teachers who stirred the people against Paul. They said Paul was fickle, proud, unimpressive in appearance and speech, dishonest, and unqualified as an apostle of Jesus Christ. Paul sent Titus, and when he returned, Paul was happy to hear the Corinthians had a change of heart.

GALATIANS:

Author: Paul

Purpose: His letter to the Galatians is a vigorous attack against the gospel of works and a defense of the gospel of faith.

Features: Blessings come from God in the faith, not law. The law declares men guilty and imprisons them; faith sets men free to enjoy liberty in Christ. Liberty is not a license. Freedoms in Christ mean freedom to produce the fruits of righteousness through a Spirit-led lifestyle.

EPHESIANS:

Author: Paul

Purpose: Letter of revelation of every spiritual blessing. A spiritual walk rooted in His spiritual wealth. "For we are His workmanship, created in Christ Jesus for good works, that we should walk in them" (Ephesians 2:10).

Features: Letter not written to confront any problem in the churches. It was sent to strengthen and encourage churches in the area.

PHILIPPIANS:

Author: Paul

Purpose: To thank the Philippians for the gift they sent to Paul while he was in prison. It was to strengthen these believers with his controlled thought that only in Christ are real unity and joy possible.

Features: Stand fast, be of the same mind, rejoice in the Lord always, but in everything by prayer and supplication and with thanksgiving. Let your requests be made known, and the peace of God, which surpasses all understanding, will guard your hearts and minds through Jesus Christ.

1 THESSALONIANS:

Author: Paul

Purpose: The church of Thessalonians was an infant church, so Paul's labors as a spiritual parent have been richly rewarded, and his affection is visible in every line of his letter.

Features: Paul encourages them to excel in their newfound faith, to increase in their love for one another, and to rejoice, pray, and give thanks always. It talks of the return of the Lord, whose advent signifies hope and comfort for the believer, both living and dead.

2 THESSALONIANS:

Author: Paul

Purpose: To renew their faith and take away destructive seeds which were spawned by false teachers regarding the coming day of the Lord.

Features: Commanding believers on their faithfulness in the midst of persecution and encouraging them that present suffering will be repaid with future glory. Paul recounts the events that must first take place, laboring for the gospel rather than lazy resignation.

1 TIMOTHY:

Author: Paul

Purpose: To give final instructions and encouragement to the church of Ephesians.

Features: A personal letter and handbook of church administration and discipline. Timothy was the young leader of the church of Ephesus.

2 TIMOTHY:

Author: Paul

Purpose: To give final instructions and encouragement to Timothy, pastor of the church of Ephesus.

Features: This is Paul's last letter from prison; it reveals his heart and his priorities—sound doctrine, steadfast faith, confident endurance, and lasting love.

TITUS:

Author: Paul

Purpose: To advise Titus, a young pastor, to set in order the church of Crete; to appoint elders, men of a proven spiritual character in their homes and businesses, to oversee the work of the church. Men and women, young and old, are to serve vital functions to fulfill the church.

Features: Stresses the necessary, practical working out of salvation in the daily lives of both the elders and the congregation. Good works are desirable and profitable for all believers.

PHILEMON:

Author: Paul

Purpose: To convince Philemon, a wealthy member of the Colossian church, to forgive his runaway slave Onesimus and to accept him as a brother in the faith.

Features: Personal letter from Paul with the confidence that brotherly love and forgiveness would prevail with Philemon and Onesimus.

HEBREWS:

Author: Unknown, but whoever it was speaks of Timothy as a "brother" (Hebrews 13:23).

Purpose: The writer of Hebrews exhorts them to "go on to perfection." He appeals to them based on the superiority of Christ over the Judaic system, better than the angels because they worship Him, better than Moses because He created him, better than the Aaronic priesthood because His sacrifice was once for all time, better than the law because He mediates a better covenant.

Features: More to be gained in Christ than to be lost in Judaism. Pressing on in Christ produces tested faith, self-discipline, and a visible love seen in good works.

JAMES:

Author: James, Jesus' half-brother, leader in the Jerusalem church

Purpose: Faith without works cannot be called faith. "Faith without works is dead" (James 2:26). To expose hypocritical practices and to teach right Christian behavior.

Features: Faith produces separation from the world and submission to God. It provides us with the ability to resist the devil and humbly draw near to God. Faith waits patiently for the coming of the Lord. Through trouble and trial, it stifles complaining.

1 PETER:

Author: Peter

Purpose: To offer encouragement to persecuted Jewish Christians to conduct themselves courageously for the person and program of Christ. Their conduct must be above reproach.

Features: Having been born again to a living hope, they are to imitate the Holy One who has called them. Fruit of that character will be conduct rooted in submission: citizens to government, servants to masters, wives to husbands, husbands to wives, and Christians to one another.

2 PETER:

Author: Peter

Purpose: To warn believers about the false teachers who are peddling damaging doctrine, so keep a close watch on your personal life.

Features: Reminding believers that although God may be longsuffering in sending judgment, ultimately, it will come. In view of that fact, believers should live lives of godliness, blamelessness, and steadfastness.

1 JOHN:

Author: Apostle John

Purpose: To let his spiritual children know to enjoy a fellowship with their God of light, love, and life.

Features: Christ's love fulfilled those qualities, and when that brand of love characterizes us, we will be free of self-condemnation and experience confidence before God.

2 JOHN:

Author: Apostle John

Purpose: To remind a chosen lady and her children who were walking in truth and faithful to the commandments from the Father, "Love one another." This is equivalent to walking with God's commandments.

Feature: We must have fellowship with God. We must have fellowship with Christians. But we must not have fellowship with false teachers.

3 JOHN:

Author: Apostle John

Purpose: To commend Gaius for his hospitality and to encourage him in his Christian life.

Features: Church leaders traveled from town to town, helping to establish new congregations. They depended on the hospitality of fellow believers like Gaius.

JUDE:

Author: Half brother of Jesus and brother of James

Purpose: To remind the church of the need for constant strong faith and to oppose heresy.

Features: We must always be on our guard about false teachers with false teachings.

REVELATION:

Author: Apostle John

Purpose: To reveal the full identity of Christ and to give warning and hope to believers.

Features: The Christians were under the persecution of Emperor Domitian (90–95 AD), and John had been exiled to the island of Patmos. John had a vision of the glorified Christ and what would take place in the future—judgment and the ultimate triumph of God over evil.

BIBLIOGRAPHY

All-In-One Bible Reference Guide, The Zondervan Corporation, 2008

Life Application Study Bible, Tyndale House Foundation, 1988, 1989, 1990, 1993, 1996, 2004, 2007

ABOUT THE AUTHOR

My name is Sandy Butcher. I am eighty years old and became a "born again Christian" in May of 2013. I was born and christened in a Methodist religion family. After I was born, we lived in a logging camp in Oregon. I spent twenty years in the small university town of Eugene, OR, with friends from grade school who are still friends today.

I met my husband, who was from the same town. We married and went to Tennessee for training because he was going overseas to Vietnam. We were young when we got married, and I believe we both knew we were not prepared to be married at eighteen years old, so the marriage ended in a divorce.

Then I met my present husband, El Butcher, at my job site. He had five children. I knew the purpose Jesus gave me was to help raise his children through their teenage years, even if I was at the young age of twenty-nine.

I know this was my purpose because I did not have any children. Later I entered the hospital to have a full hysterectomy only to find my own reproductive organs had grown together, so I would never have had my own children.

Because of my circumstances, it is my belief that Jesus gave me the purpose to raise my stepchildren. I dearly love these children as my own. My husband has since passed away from dementia. I stayed, and I took care of him; for better or worse, God means for us to fulfill our marriage vows.

We had a horse boarding facility which, of course, I had to take care of after my husband passed. It was our retirement. It was not easy to work feeding twenty-eight horses, performing all necessary repairs, and making the decisions to keep us profitable. After my husband died, a girl came to the barn and led me back to Jesus. Also, another girl who rode one of my horses helped me find a church in my area. Oddly, she did not plan to go to the church she had me attend. It was a small church with a membership of about two hundred people.

I met these two girls who led me to salvation, and my baptism was in July of 2013. I had known God and Jesus from my childhood Sunday school Bible studies, where we put bunnies on charts as a reward. We sang the song "Jesus Loves Me," and I went to summer Bible studies. I wanted to know everything right away about God, Jesus, and the Bible. I had such a deep love that I started what I thought would help me meet my goal quicker. If I would have had access to quicker teachings, I know my goals would have come along faster, and I would not have been so confused. I want to help you so you will get a quicker picture of our obedience to God, following Jesus, and listening to the Holy Spirit.